AUGUST AND RAB

AUGUST AND RAB

A MEMOIR

Mollie Butler

WEIDENFELD AND NICOLSON · LONDON

*For my six children, who told me to write it
and who helped me to do so,
this memoir with my love*

CONTENTS

ILLUSTRATIONS

(Between pages 84 and 85)

ACKNOWLEDGEMENTS

I am greatly indebted to three dear friends, Mr Peter Goldman CBE, Dr Robert Robson of Trinity College, Cambridge, and the Reverend H. A. Williams of the Community of the Resurrection, for their wise advice concerning this book.

Sir John Verney read my manuscript and patiently corrected faults of taste or grammar; I offer him my deepest gratitude.

Rab's sister, Mrs Dorothy Middleton, and Mr Anthony Howard, his biographer, have answered many of my queries about writing a book. Mrs Gertrud Watson typed the manuscript with zeal and kindness. My agent, Miss Felicity Bryan, was fiercely energetic in finding me a publisher, and Miss Alex MacCormick took me under her excellent editorial wing. I thank them all.

I should also like to thank, for their permission to quote them, Mr Kenneth Harris, Sir Nicholas Henderson, Mr James Lees-Milne, the Countess of Longford, Baroness Macleod of Borve for permission to quote the late Mr Iain Macleod, the Rt Hon. Mr Enoch Powell, Mr R. D. Thorpe, Mr J. A. Weir, Mr Nicholas Wollaston and Mr Philip Ziegler. I am grateful to Faber & Faber for permission to quote from 'Musée des beaux arts' by W. H. Auden; and to A. P. Watt Ltd on behalf of Michael B. Yeats and Macmillan & Co. for permission to quote from 'The Pity of Love' by W. B. Yeats.

My daughters Mrs Perina Fordham and Mrs Susie Hamilton have shown an enthusiasm which has spurred me on from start to finish. They have helped me more than anyone with both practical and literary suggestions, and my gratitude to them is immense.

1

FROM QUIET HOMES
AND FIRST BEGINNING

'When my father was in prison,' I used to say, waiting rather unkindly perhaps for the look of embarrassment this remark would evoke. He was taken prisoner in the Battle of Loos at the beginning of the First World War. Pam and I were six and seven at the time and I do not remember much before that, beyond scattered images, *disjecta membra*. If I push my mind to the horizon of consciousness, I see a child toiling up a shingle beach and, on reaching the top, being filled with rapture by the glitter of the sea. I use the word now, but at the time of which I write the child did not, of course, know that the clutch at the heart she experienced on seeing sunlight dancing on water would be so described. For over seventy years this sensation of pleasure has stayed with me and is recalled by merely hearing the scrunch of pebbles, which I find more exciting on a beach than sand.

Another faint picture is of the coronation procession of King George v in 1910, when I was three years old. My great-uncle had a house in Carlton House Terrace, from which the view of the Mall must have been splendid, but not a rack remains to me except the sensation of satisfaction that I had been allowed to come, while Pam was judged too young and had to stay at home.

The 1914 war, which we are told brought an end to a world we have never known, impressed even my childish mind. I heard my father say, 'Frank [the butcher's boy in our village] has gone; I must go too.' The words meant little to me at the time, though I can vividly recall looking out of the nursery window as I heard them. My father was then forty-one years old and need not have joined the young men being called up, but he was intensely patriotic and conventional (I do not assume that the words are synonymous) and asked his old friend Colonel Romer of the Buffs Regiment for a commission.

My mother took Pam and me to some strange amorphous place of pine trees and trenches called Blackdown Camp to be near him, and from here we saw him off to the Front. I see the train bearing him away even now, with women and children waving goodbye, and feel again the solemnity with which I accompanied my parents to Evensong on the night before his departure. There was a Communion service at the end and I felt full of awe, sitting at the back of the church while they went up to the altar.

The night we heard my father was missing Pam had an attack of colitis, from which she suffered, and I felt a childish indignation for my poor mother having to carry her wailing around the bedroom when her mind must have been filled with dreadful anxiety. Strangely enough, clear as the memory of that night remains, I have no recollection of hearing the news of his safety as a prisoner.

During the war years my mother had some freakish idea that it would be good for us to live by the sea, and so we moved to Cliftonville, a suburb of Margate of quite exceptional ugliness, with rows of hideous villas, their blue slate roofs shining in the rain. We had a variety of governesses and, though my sister and I were two very mild and ordinary children, the governesses seemed frequently to depart, and I do not remember anything of what they tried to teach us. One of them had been at a great house, Knole. We never tired of her stories about the little girl who was her charge, nor imagined how famous Vita Sackville-West was to become. The last governess was a friend. She played the piano and I used to sit beneath my mother's Broadwood, laying the foundations of a life-long love of music. In after years I found music was drink to me in the way that literature was food. Miss Hendy, our governess, had a brother called Philip of unimaginable beauty (Pam and I both fell in love with him), who later became Director of the National Gallery and incurred much criticism when he started the idea of having the pictures cleaned. It was said that he was under the influence of a German crank who persuaded him to do this.

Back in our village, we shared a French governess with the Barrington children at a neighbouring house called Little Bookham Manor, where, strangely, Rab stayed as a boy with his cousins the Meredith Townsends, who had lived there before the Barringtons.

Patrick, the present Lord Barrington, has always worn his nose a very slight fraction out of straight after running headlong into my sister during a game of hide-and-seek; it was said that the impact pushed his cartilage to one side. We spent hours sitting on the ground of Bookham Common painting the blue Surrey distance. Mademoiselle was very scornful of our efforts, though Pam and I rather fancied our watercolour sketches. Our own village had a sort of Cranford quality: a long dusty street with no motor traffic and many old ladies, with whom we were bidden to tea. The vicarage boys were our close companions, Felix who was Pam's ally and John who was mine, and we spent happy hours chasing each other with water-pistols filled from the wooden butt outside the garden door.

We moved about in a pony cart pulled by Pilgrim, who meant nothing to me, and a yellow whicker donkey carriage, to which was attached beloved Bess. On picnics she would be taken from the shafts and would lie on her side with her eyes shut, opening her mouth meanwhile and displaying enormous yellow teeth, between which I would place a luscious pear.

Occasionally my mother would take us to London, untroubled by bombs in spite of the war, to stay with an indulgent cousin who had been in the Indian Civil Service and whose dining-room walls were hung with tiger skins, their beautiful heads mounted and their mouths open. We were allowed to feed them. On one unforgettable visit he took us to a pantomime on two afternoons running. All that comes back to me is of two comedians sitting under a chestnut tree and whenever one of them told a lie a chestnut would fall on his head. One of them said, 'Lloyd George says he knows when the war is going to end,' whereupon the whole tree erupted and covered the stage with nuts.

My father had an alarming cousin, Clara Vincent, with whom we also used to stay during the war at D'Abernon Lodge in Surrey. It was a large house with a large staff of servants who assembled, as was the custom in those days, for family prayers before breakfast, to which the children also came. As I knelt by my chair facing the wall I felt my head suddenly clutched by claws and realized that the parrot had got out of its cage. My terror of Cousin Clara kept me rigid until prayers were over, when I was praised by everyone for my apparent bravery; they did not know that it was not the parrot which had caused my fear.

On my father's return from Germany he decided that his war years had been too easy and that he must now 'do his bit'. He had been at Fürstenberg and Gütersloh, far from the mud and carnage of Flanders, had been considered too old to try and escape, and had spent much of his time stage-managing plays amongst the other prisoners. They wore dressing-up garments sent by my mother through the Red Cross. Conditions in prison had been comparatively comfortable and he now made up his mind to go mine-sweeping. This gallant decision removed him from our lives once more, but while in prison he had decided that he wanted to own a chicken farm and my mother set about looking for a suitable venue. This was found at a dear, shabby old house in Essex called Great Codham Hall (all houses in Essex are 'Halls'). Codham was a house of respectable antiquity; it is mentioned briefly in Morant's *History and Antiquities in the County of Essex* published in 1768, where we read that a certain Catharine who became the wife of William Spencer in 1623 brought with her the Manor of Great Codham Hall. 'His [William Spencer's] grandson sold the estate to Sir Richard Pyne, Lord Chief Justice of Ireland: that entailed it on his grandson Henry Pyne Esq. and his heirs male. But the latter, unwisely losing his life in a duel on 28 February 1712, and having only daughters, Great Codham Hall fell to the heirs of his sister.'

Whether the unwise Henry stayed to haunt the house is not known, though I certainly once saw a figure who proved not to be there. I glanced up casually from the piano and, through the open drawing-room door, saw someone, but on going into the hall to investigate, I found it empty . . . From Morant's *History* one would have expected a house of some distinction, but Codham had none. One walked straight into a large hall, from which a flight of shallow oak stairs led up to a very ordinary first floor of no architectural pretensions. But my father, with his passion for pulling houses about, discovered two very beautiful wide-arched open fireplaces of late Tudor bricks in the hall and drawing-room. Beside the fireplace in the hall was a concealed space which we all hoped had been a priest's hide-out.

I learnt to love the surrounding countryside. Essex is supposed to be flat and indeed the land as it nears London is dismally so, but round us were delicious steep lanes and undulating pastures. It is elm country and those noble trees guarded our home and reared themselves in the hedges.

The colours are very sparse in late summer; the elms become indigo blue and the stubble fields turn to pale gold, while the heat often drains nearly all colour from the sky, where the great clouds pile themselves against the very faintest blue. There were nightingales in those days, not only at night-time, for sometimes at midday there would come a burst of rippling song from the deeps of a wood. But not even a nightingale's voice was so exciting as the first chatter of the returning swallows, who for me forever herald the magic of the coming summer.

Our education, such as it was, took place at a day school on Wimbledon Common, run by two old ladies called Miss Farman and Miss Sidford, the former having taught my mother. She wore academic dress and a headgear which made her look like the poet Dante, but I doubt if she was entitled to any of it. I was grateful to Miss Carter, who taught me the rudiments of Latin, which later helped me with English words ('You all know what an aperient is – remember *aperire* means "to open" ') and even more grateful to Miss Hughes, who fed my love of English Literature. We lived in term time with my dear, deaf grandmother, Mrs Napier, in a tall, forbidding house just off the Common. Next door lived Sir Fenton Aylmer, who had won the vc for sliding down a wire rope from a bridge in India to rescue a comrade, cutting off half his hand thereby. He was always very kind when Pam and I went round to find a tennis ball which had gone over his garden wall. They were ugly, respectable houses and it was a relief to go back to the countryside round our Essex home.

Here my sister and I were to do the rest of our growing up, greatly assisted by periodic visits to Italy. Our uncle Alan Napier was British Consul in Venice, and here we went, travelling, as was normal in those days, in the Orient Express, under the supposed care of the King's Messenger. Sixty years ago the Messenger travelled by train in a carriage to himself, surrounded by bags of presumably important and confidential papers, and he naturally never set eyes on the two ignorant girls who were part of his baggage.

In a long life Venice has never disappointed me, but in those days it was a paradise. The Napiers lived in the *piano nobile* of a house on the Fondamenta Bonlini. Above them lived the formidable Mrs Somers Cocks who, though stone deaf, travelled all over the world since she could lip-read in several languages, even Chinese, it was reported. In this enchanting home we meet the English-speaking colony. Leslie Hartley comes to lunch with my aunt. He is quite young, but already a well-known writer, and I watch, fascinated by his plummy voice and by the hand with which he gesticulates and to which a morsel of pudding adheres. He is plump, but has a touch of the sinister, which is apparent in his writing. Years later he tells me that he has put me into one of his books. He takes us out on the lagoon in his gondola piloted by himself and his handsome gondolier, Pietro (who also comes into his writings), and far out on the pearly waters I have a sense of agoraphobia in this long thin boat. My uncle takes us to a music party in the vast Palazzo of the Princesse de Polignac. She is terrifying, grey-haired, authoritative and dismissive. My sister and I shrink into the background, intensely aware of our own unworthiness, but cheer up when Jimmie Smith plays jazz on the Princesse's piano.

Opposite my uncle, across the canal, lived Prince and Princess Clary, Alphy and Lidi, in total penury. They were Austrian, had lost all their possessions in the war, knew or were related to all the nearly crowned heads in Europe and were two of the dearest and most popular people in Venetian society. They were excessively good company and Pam and I hung on their lips when, in perfect English, they told stories from their past.

We were lucky beyond belief in that our aunt was a wonderful guide and never rested until we revelled as absolutely as herself in Carpaccio or marvelled at the then totally black Tintorettos in the Scuola di San Rocco.

To this day, when I hear Italian spoken, a feeling of happiness steals over me, the sun shines and I hear the harsh bells from San Trovaso at the back of my uncle's garden, or I am in Harry's Bar being 'treated' by an officer from one of the ships of the Mediterranean Fleet, which paid an official call on the Consul whenever they lay off Venice. Naval pinnaces would come alongside the steps of the Piazzetta of St Mark's to take us out for parties on board, and my uncle and aunt would entertain the favourites in return.

My uncle was only once known to lose his imperturbability. He was meeting, in his official capacity, the ship in which Sir Percy Loraine, our Minister in Teheran, was travelling on his way back to England. Somehow this rather 'difficult' diplomat managed to fall from the landing steps into the very dirty waters of the Guidecca between the ship and the waterside. Aunt Dor was startled when my uncle returned demanding an instant hot bath and clean clothes for the much put-out

Sir Percy who, dripping wet, was following in a state of shock and in mortal fear of what he might have swallowed from the polluted Venetian water.

My father and mother were the dearest and most unworldly people, but totally unbusinesslike. They were both descended from Lowland Scottish families (he a Montgomerie and she a Napier), a race that is supposed to be hard-headed and shrewd, but these qualities were lacking in them and the chicken farm was a failure. Money, never plentiful in our family, became scarce. There was none for theatres or concerts in London, and my music-loving was nourished vicariously by reading Francis Toye's reviews of concerts in the *Morning Post*, the only newspaper that my father considered sufficiently Conservative to have in the house.

However, as we grew older, Pam and I were allowed to venture into the arts as provided by the great world. She took lessons in modelling in clay, at which she excelled, and I joined the London Philharmonic Choir. Oh, that I could have played an instrument, but I had only my voice. We were rehearsed by Kennedy Scott at a dim hall in Eccleston Square behind Victoria Station, where I sang amongst the sopranos beside my long-time friend Ursula Bowlby, a real musician, while I was only a feeble music-lover. Our great moment came when the Choir was chosen to sing at one of the Courtauld-Sargent Concerts in the Queen's Hall. Klemperer was to conduct us in the Beethoven Choral Ninth Symphony. He came to one of the rehearsals, a raven-haired god-like creature. Years later I saw him as a very old man conducting *Fidelio* at Covent Garden; he was obliged to conduct sitting down and some affliction prevented him from shutting his mouth, but the magic was still there.

My first visit to Covent Garden took place when I was twenty-two years old, and August Courtauld took me to a performance of *The Meistersingers*. In those days everyone wore full evening dress for the opera, the men in white ties and the women *décolletées*. The brilliance of this scene, combined with Wagner's heady music, left an ineradicable impression.

August Courtauld was a neighbour of ours in Essex; he was three years older than I and, though his sister Betty was a friend of mine, he himself was something of a mystery, totally unlike the other young men whom I met and danced with. August didn't like dancing; he preferred

7

wild-fowling and was constantly away on expeditions to the Arctic or to Africa, from where he wrote to me in tea since the ink had run out. But what he really preferred to anything was going to sea in his small racing yacht *Duet*. He took Pam and me on one occasion and we got stuck on the mud, of which there is a great deal in the Thames Estuary, remaining there until the rising tide floated us off and we were able to return to my terrified parents at four in the morning.

Years later, when August and I were married, he found another, bigger yacht, which he renamed *Duet*, and she became and still is almost a member of the family.

I had known August on and off since I was twelve years old. It is difficult to stand back and describe anybody with whom one has grown up; they are part of the fabric of life. He was very handsome with a lively dark-skinned face, black hair and eyebrows, and expressive green eyes. He was a romantic who would have been at home in the time of Queen Elizabeth I, charting unknown seas, for he was a brilliant navigator and it was, from his point of view, a sort of tragedy that so little of the earth's surface was left unexplored.

He had enormous courage, both of the kind which recognizes danger and is prepared to meet it, and also that different courage which knows no fear. This could make his company frightening at times, especially in his boat carrying full sail, when he was happiest. He had disliked his public school, Charterhouse, and swore that no son of his should go there. He scorned the passion for organized games which was so prevalent in his youth; to get out of them he took up shooting and was in the school team, remaining an excellent shot all his life.

While at Cambridge August must have impressed his college, Trinity, in some way since, when I arrived there forty years later, the Head Porter, who had worked in the Buttery in August's day, was able to show me his old rooms. Here he and his friends had given tea parties for their dogs which, being disallowed in college, were hauled up to the windows from the Great Court in suitcases or cricket bags. (I cannot believe that this rather Bertie Wooster scene was typical of undergraduate life in the 1920s.)

August and I, in different parties, had met and danced together at a Trinity May Ball. Afterwards, instead of the usual romantic drift in a punt, he had taken me to see the College kitchens. Although I had no notion of this at the time, these dated from 1605, and the enormously high-pitched ceiling was black with the smoke of centuries which used to make its way out of a lantern in the roof. There was a vast fireplace, where a spit was turned by the heat from the fire below it, and hanging on the walls were bright copper utensils which were still in use. I had to admit that it was as picturesque as floating on the river.

August was a strange mixture of eccentricity and the conventional. Conventional in his love of music: he loved Chopin, Bach and Beethoven, but I doubt if he would have listened even to Debussy. He loved reading, but would have drawn the line at *Ulysses* or the works of Jean-Paul Sartre. His eccentricity took the form of an almost total lack of regard for the orthodoxy of ordinary behaviour. When he was a member of the Essex County Council, someone from the opposing group cast doubts on the honesty of the Conservatives in the Council; August was on his feet in a moment. 'Anyone who doubts the good faith of those on our side can meet me in the car-park when business is over,' he declared in quietly belligerent tones. The remark was withdrawn at once.

He had very good manners before women, never using a swear word in their company, but he thought nothing of going out to dinner with dirty fingernails.

When I was twenty, he decided to test me as a companion for life by inviting me to join him on the west coast of Scotland in an old Bristol pilot cutter which he shared with a Cambridge friend, Frank Carr. Accordingly my sailing chaperone, Avis Hodgson, and I went on board *Cariad* at Ullapool on Loch Broom in August 1928, and I had my initiation into what was to become a long life of cruising. I had only sailed on the Norfolk Broads before. I had also never been so far north in Scotland and was captivated by its wild beauty. Life on board was tough. August's only companion was an old bosun, and Avis and I were expected to work alongside him in the galley or on deck, and if *Cariad* dragged her anchor, which she did at 4 a.m. in Tobermory harbour, we were commanded on deck in our nightclothes to help pull her into deeper water. It was exciting as well as being tough, but I minded the shortage of fresh water on board, since August decided we must use our ration for washing twice over. I suppose it was churlish to be fastidious about such details amid scenery of sovereign beauty, but looking back I am not really surprised that, having passed my test, I said no. Next year

August tried again, on land this time, and the following year I came to realize my own blind stupidity and we became engaged.

The Courtauld family are descended from the Huguenots of that name and came from La Rochelle in the Ile d'Oléron, from where they escaped after the revocation of the Edict of Nantes and came to England as refugees in 1685. Much of their stern, puritan blood ran in August's veins and I discovered after our marriage that some of the Courtauld aunts, had they lived at the time of the Civil War, would have been on the side of Oliver Cromwell. I liked to think that our own children had also the blood of my Scottish ancestors, who had fought for Charles I and later for Charles II in exile.

But, before we were married, a great drama took place. This has been described by Nicholas Wollaston in an excellent book called *The Man on the Ice Cap*.

In 1930, when we finally became engaged, August had already arranged to go on an expedition to Greenland in July of that year. This was the British Arctic Air-Route Expedition led by Gino Watkins and consisting of a party of young men who found in this idea of discovering the shortest air-route to the West a wonderful excuse for their desire to visit Greenland and explore places still blank on the map. (It is a fact that planes regularly flying on this Polar route between England, Canada and America, are profiting by August's and Gino's ideas of long ago.)

I had no knowledge of the Arctic in those days and, apart from my natural sorrow at losing August for a year (as I thought) so soon after becoming engaged to him, I had no qualms for his safety. He had returned twice before from expeditions to Greenland while up at Cambridge and, though this was a longer and more ambitious affair, my ignorance precluded anxiety. I never dreamt that he would become an international hero before I saw him again.

Thus, when the news arrived on 23 April the following year that his ice-cap station could not be found and that there were fears for his safety, it came as an unimaginable blow. It was brought home to me in a flash that I was no more immune from terror than anyone else.

What happened was as follows. The expedition set up an ice-cap station about 130 miles inland from their seashore base camp with the intention of keeping weather recordings throughout the year. Their instruments measured temperature, pressure, wind force, speed of clouds, etc. The idea was for two men at a time to spend a month at this

10

lonely occupation, being relieved by a further two men, and so on. This was the idea, but the reality was very different.

No one had ever travelled on the ice-cap in winter, where conditions were ferocious with constant blizzards, during which travel was impossible. The men were forced to huddle together in their tent for warmth. The dogs outside had only their noses showing above the snow, and later it would be found that they had eaten the leather harness with which they were attached to the sledges. Consequently, the relief of the ice-cap station became more and more difficult. When it came to the turn of August and his companion, a party set off from the base camp on 26 October and took thirty-nine days to travel the 130 miles, so terrible were the conditions. The sledges bearing precious food and instruments constantly overturned and broke on the rough ice, while men with frost-bitten fingers toiled to mend them. I quote from August's diary: 'Still blowing, tent shaking and beating all day. Towards evening the wind increased in violence and as darkness fell the tent was thundering and shaking as if it would be torn to pieces at any moment. Had to shout to make myself heard by Hampton who was only a foot away. Everything covered with rime and snow. Sleeping bags wet. We slept in our clothes and prayed the tent would stay up.' And again, 'We hadn't been a quarter of a mile before all the sledges were over. The surface was alternately knife-edge drifts as hard as concrete and soft snow.'

They had never imagined an Arctic winter could be so vicious, and, when they finally arrived at the ice-cap station in a temperature of 45° below zero, the two resident occupants had been there for two months rather then one. August decided it was impossible to continue the plan of relieving the station under such appalling conditions; another plan must be resorted to and he had just this plan. He would stay alone on the ice-cap with as much food as could be spared by the returning party and continue to keep observations for the rest of the winter. He told Freddie Chapman that, with books, and a good supply of tobacco and food, he would be perfectly happy. Chapman and the others were understandably anxious, but what was the alternative? Impossible to make this journey during the bad months, and the food which should have kept two men at the station had been partially consumed during the long haul they had just come through, which had taken so much longer than planned. Thus August's courageous offer was accepted and he was left on 5 December. He was to remain alone, although he did not know it then, until he was rescued, literally dug out, on 5 May of the following year.

He wrote, after the others had gone, 'The silence outside was almost terrible. Nothing to hear but one's heart beating and the blood ticking in one's veins.' His tent, at an altitude of 9,000 feet, was a canvas dome ten feet across and six feet high, which was hung by tapes from a frame of curved bamboo ribs. A ventilator pipe went up from the top and an outer tent hung over the whole. Here August would dress up every three hours and crawl through the tunnel to take readings from his instruments outside, constantly having to unblock the tunnel with his frost-bitten fingers and toes from the snow which ceaselessly filled it. Inside his tent he read the books which had been left by previous occupants, as well as his own: *Guy Mannering, Moby Dick, Jane Eyre* and his favourite Joseph Conrad. He planned the perfect boat for when he got home, played chess against himself, thought up the meals he would have when food was once more not just a question of pemmican and pea flour, and wrote messages to me in his diary.

No doubt the same routine would have remained through his five months ordeal, but on 22 March disaster overtook him. A gale blew, the snow drifted, the hole through which he crawled was covered. He had kept an empty ration-box on top of the hole to prevent this happening, but such was the weight of frozen snow on top of the box that he could no longer push it up; he was completely buried. Here August showed his almost superhuman quality. His paraffin for light and warmth was nearly finished so that he was forced to lie most of the time in the dark, waiting for release. Nicholas Wollaston writes:

His ability to adapt to circumstances – itself a kind of modesty – was one of the qualities most needed to bring him through, as important as self-discipline, emotional stability and courage . . . Anticipation can be a killer. And hope diminishes as the fact of abandonment grows. In stories of survival Wilfred Noyce notes a common element, 'a sense of self in community', a belief in the encouragement and co-operation of others, that buoyed a man's spirit. So it was with August Courtauld. Always, to supplement his capacity for endurance, there was a feeling of belonging to the expedition, of community with friends, as if a thin connection ran back like a vein down the line of half-mile flags from the ice-cap station to to the coast. Knowing that the others were at the base, and trusting them to come back for him as soon as they could, helped to sustain him . . . 'No man is an island, entire of itself' even in the middle of the Greenland ice-cap.

His tent was now very cold, 'the walls, bulging inward from the weight of snow, were lined with hoar frost that hung in icicles, reducing the space still further; they drifted and pieces dropped on him in the dark. Condensation turned to ice in his sleeping bag, so that his feet froze and he had to warm them with his hands.' As I quote Nicholas Wollaston's description of his plight, even after more than half a century, tears come to my eyes. August was down to two ounces of food a day, and yet he could write in his diary:

But as each month passed without relief I felt more and more certain of its arrival. By the time I was snowed in I had no doubts on the matter, which was a great comfort to my mind. I will not attempt any explanation of this but leave it as a fact, which was very clear to me during that time, that while powerless to help myself, some outer force was in action on my side, and I wasn't fated to leave my bones on the Greenland ice-cap.

What joy and relief he must have felt when Gino and the others literally cut him free on 5 May.

The first search party had set out from the base camp on 1 March, but, being unable to find the drifted-over ice-cap station, had returned, and it was their report which triggered the terrifying message home.

Gino immediately set off with two others and three sledges on 21 April, with the result that we know. In the meanwhile, the warning had been picked up by the press and the story became world news. Waiting at home, my mother, who must have feared just as much as I did that the impossible could happen and that he would not be found, was a wonderful comfort to me during those weeks, until miraculously on 8 May came the lifting of the burden, when we heard he was safe.

But that terrible time has left me scarred for life. I always expect the worst and, however often the worst does not happen, I still remain incurably fearful.

> The cold wet winds ever blowing
> And the shadowy hazel-grove
> Where mouse-gray waters are flowing
> Threaten the head that I love.

Yeats's head is singular, but mine are many, and as the heads increased so did my anxieties.

August and the expedition happily returned that winter of 1931. His exploits having received world-wide attention from the press, he was now something of a lion, with invitations from the great and the good, which he steadily refused – sometimes to my disappointment.

We were married on 2 January 1932 in Southwark Cathedral, and set off for a honeymoon which was to last three months and more. We had a wonderful send-off from Victoria Station, with placards in chalk saying 'Courtauld departure from Platform so-and-so'. As we arrived at Dover Station that dark and windy January night, the ticket collector said softly, 'I hope you won't be taking the lady to the Arctic, sir.'

2

OUT TO THE
UNDISCOVERED ENDS

The most remarkable part of our honeymoon was spent in the Sudan, in those days the Anglo-Egyptian Sudan. Charles de Bunsen, who had been a friend of August when they were both up at Trinity College, was now a District Commissioner in the Sudanese province of Kordofan; he had invited August and me to accompany him on trek.

Before doing so, we visited Colonel Boustead, who commanded the Sudan Camel Corps in Khartoum and was later to fight against the Italians in Abyssinia. He was a small, choleric, but charming man, who had been an old flame of my mother. He readily supplied us with camels, explaining rather sternly that they must be properly fed so that their humps would be as fat on return as they were now. Alas, in the event, when he got them back, he did not think their curves were sufficiently rounded and we were reprimanded. Mine was a proper riding, as opposed to baggage, camel from the Red Sea. I do not remember its sex, but it was white in colour and well trained in the complicated business of collapsing its huge frame on to the ground to allow me to mount and dismount.

Going on trek with Charles was a marvellous experience and we did it in great comfort with Arab servants whose care and courtesy surpassed anything I have ever known. We usually slept on camp beds under the stars and in the morning there might be small paw marks in the sand round where we had lain. I would wake to the loud grumbling of the baggage camels being loaded up in the dark to go ahead of us, and later a hand as black as the darkness all round would pass me a cup of very sweet tea as I lay in my sleeping bag. Gradually, as I dressed, the sun would come up and we would mount our camels and ride towards breakfast at the next camp. I shall never forget the beauty of those early morning rides, the freshness of the air, the great pink and blue skies above the endless stretches of sand, broken by the patchy scrub on which perched pale doves. As we rode, two Egyptian soldiers from the Camel Corps rode before us, one with a Union Jack and the other with the flag of Egypt, which they would raise if we passed so much as one human being on our way. Our camp would be spread ready, a delicious breakfast and, even more delicious, baths in canvas containers awaiting us. How water was produced for these I cannot think, but there they were, and on a camp table, reverently laid out as though by the most experienced lady's maid, all my cosmetics and our hair brushes – an altar raised to the completeness of the toilette.

During the heat of the day Charles would dispense justice to the villagers; he was their ruler and they took his word as literal law. I remember one day of particularly stifling heat we lunched in a tent, as our camp had no shade. The cook – I will call him Abdul – produced hot soup made from Bovril. Charles, disgusted, said that if ever such a thing happened again, he and Abdul would have to part. With great dignity Abdul replied that Allah would never allow Charles and himself to part. In the evening, we might move on again, and the process would be repeated, only this time it would be the light of the supper table towards which we rode. It was an idyllic visit in conditions which have disappeared for ever. (Charles later married Margaret Babington-Smith, who became one of my dearest friends.)

We returned to England by way of Istanbul and Venice in mid-April. It was raining in London and my dear father-in-law detailed for us the number of people who had died in our absence.

I became devoted to my father-in-law, Samuel Augustine Courtauld. He was a shy, quiet millionaire who did enormous good with his money, particularly in the fields of medicine and education, and was quite content to lead a dull and rather obscure life compared to his more flamboyant Courtauld relations. He was old-fashioned, hated publicity and viewed the modern world with a fastidious distaste. He moved happily between his two large houses, one in Essex and the other in Palace Green, Kensington, where nobody of interest ever came. He and my mother-in-law never entertained anyone from the world of the arts or of the intellect or even the social life of London. And yet he was a most civilized and highly educated man who would sit by his fireside in the evening absorbed in Horace in the original Latin, annotating with a gold pencil as he read. He had two cars and two chauffeurs, and he and his wife drove out separately on their humdrum ways. At home, too, they sat separately, he in his library and she in her drawing-room. He was a great reader and he and I shared a love for the works of Jane Austen and P. G. Wodehouse, and we would talk over our favourite passages for hours at a time. He once said to me, 'As chairman of the Governors of Felsted School, I often have to seek eminent persons to give away the prizes on speech day. I have sometimes thought how splendid it would have been to find somebody of the calibre of Gussy Fink-Nottle to liven up the proceedings, as he did, in an inebriated state, at Market Snodsborough Grammar School.' He had a quiet but strong sense of humour, which it was my joy to arouse. If I have made him seem dull, I have failed, for he was not that.

Life with August was to consist very largely of life at sea. Already that summer of 1932 found us sailing in *Duet* on the west coast of Scotland – the perfect cruising ground, which we were to return to many times. I learned to love life for six weeks at a time in a small boat, for *Duet* was indeed small as a home. After a day being buffeted in storm and rain, it was wonderful to sit round the cabin table having supper in a calm anchorage. I even learned to go without a bath except on the rare occasions when we went ashore to an hotel. On one occasion, moored at the head of Loch Broom, August mistook a private house for an hotel. He thought that the group of men standing outside the front door were hotel guests, instead of guns about to set off grouse shooting, and going inside to ask for a pint of bitter, he received a rude shock.

It was a life of stimulating contrasts, and the beauty of islands and mountains, of sea birds, who swam beside us, and northern sunsets, even sometimes northern lights, were enormous rewards. But I was often very frightened. To begin with, I was ignorant of seafaring terms and, leaving me alone at the tiller, August would shout, 'For God's sake *luff* or we shall be on those rocks.' I very soon learned to distinguish cause and effect. I also learned that, when the water looked liquid, we should have fine weather and that a solid-seeming sea meant the opposite.

Our first home ashore to which I moved that autumn was a furnished house in Chelsea. Meanwhile August, with the aid of my father and our skipper, Jack Bedford, was bringing *Duet* home from the west coast of Scotland to her berth on the south east coast of England. I was excused this long passage since I was to have my first child in a month or two. Perina was born in December, rather to the resentment of Sir John Maude, the owner of the furnished house. He telephoned to say, 'I see you had a baby in my house,' in tones of deep displeasure. When she grew older, Perina disliked *Duet* (had she resented those weeks afloat before she was born?) and used to punish her dolls by saying, 'I shall send you on the boat if you are naughty.' But Christopher, who was born in 1934, and Julien, who followed on 1 January 1938, seemed to have salt water in their veins and crewed for their father in all weathers. August taught Christopher to be a very fine navigator; Christopher took *Duet* to the Mediterranean during one of his Cambridge vacations, bringing her back across the notorious Bouche du Rhone in bad weather to meet a deadline when his three brothers – Julien, on leave from National Service, Stephen and William, still schoolboys – and I were arriving to join him at Gibraltar for a cruise to Lisbon. His bad weather had also been ours; after a flight from England so rough that the plane's lavatory door fell off its hinges, we touched down an hour late, whilst an oilskin-clad Christopher stood on the tarmac pointing reproachfully at his watch.

To return to 1934, the year of Christopher's birth. August's passionate love of the Arctic was drawing him back, and he suggested I should go with him the following year to Greenland, where he had an idea of climbing a range of mountains which had been sighted from the Tiger Moth of the 1930–31 expedition. These mountains were higher than any seen in the Arctic before and had been named after Gino Watkins, who had been killed in Greenland in 1932. The French and Italians had both tried to climb them and failed, and August decided to try and climb them himself. He invited Jack Longland (now Sir Jack), an experienced climber who had been on Mount Everest, Professor Lawrence Wager, a climber who had been with him in Greenland, and his brother Hal Wager, to join him in a new expedition to conquer the Watkins mountains. These three men were also to bring their wives, and we should be the first white women to land on the east coast of Greenland. It was a terrific wrench to leave my two small children for the summer, but the chance was too great to miss, and on 4 July 1935 we sailed from Aberdeen Harbour in the Norwegian sealing ship *Quest*, Sir Ernest Shackleton's old ship, on board which he died. The captain and crew were Norwegians and we were to pick up three Danish members of the expedition in Iceland. One of them, Ebbe Munck, was later to become a national hero in Denmark for leading the resistance movement against the Germans in World War II. As we sailed out of Aberdeen the harbour master shouted, 'Where are you bound for?' and back from the pilot came the single magic word, 'Greenland.'

Nowadays people fly back and forth to those parts as easily as they do to Europe, but fifty years ago it was still an adventure. It was also extremely uncomfortable. The *Quest* had a rounded bottom to prevent her being crushed in pack-ice, and this meant that she rolled at sea abominably. I myself saw the instrument on the bridge register a roll of thirty-five degrees before retiring with all haste to my bunk, and Jack Longland has written that he saw forty degrees. The seas between Iceland and Greenland have the reputation of being some of the worst in the world, and for two days the ship was flung about by angry black waves the roar of which was accentuated by the hideous shrieking of Arctic winds. But on the evening of the third day it grew calmer and next morning the ship, on an even keel, was steaming between snow-white ice floes, on which the sun sparkled. They stretched away on an equally sparkling sea to where, all along the horizon, lay our goal, the mountains of Greenland. The beauty of the scene and the joy and relief with which we viewed it were intense.

This serene fairyland, where it never grew dark at this time of year, was, however, to show a very different face that evening. At 9 p.m. we were faced with having to abandon ship. We were caught in brash ice (small, tightly packed, yet insubstantial bits of ice) and unable to navigate while a current was pushing us towards a huge iceberg. The captain came down from the crow's nest and said there was no more to be done; if the iceberg hit the ship, all would be lost. It was not a happy prospect as the coast was still thirty miles away and the brash ice looked most inhospitable and unsuitable for landing on. However, we all worked at getting blankets, tents and food on deck and then waited helpless while the ship was swept inexorably onwards. As it approached midnight, with the moon and the sun both visible in a calm and beautiful sky, we passed the huge towering berg by a few feet and were safe. We celebrated with cocoa. Looking back fifty years later, I cannot think why we did not drink anything stronger.

This adventure, which might so easily have turned to tragedy, was the last of its kind and the rest of our two months were spent in a happy isolation from the anxieties and rumours which troubled Europe that summer of 1935.

It was noticeable how the *Quest*, so cramped and insignificant in Aberdeen harbour, enlarged herself into a home; indeed, she became more like an hotel, when fourteen Eskimos came on board and camped on deck, accompanied by fourteen husky dogs, who were penned up in the bows. Dogs and humans all wished for a lift further up the coast. But first we landed at Angmagsalik and were given a rapturous welcome by the Eskimos who remembered August from five years ago. In those days there were only four wooden buildings at this east coast settlement: the church, the Danish Lutheran pastor's house, a primitive wireless station and the shop. Everyone else, during the summer, lived in sealskin tents. The Eskimos are the most hospitable people imaginable, and we were invited constantly to their tents, where I found our visits something of an ordeal as the weather was hot and in every tent stood large open containers filled with urine, in which the women washed their hair.

Our journey up the beautiful coast was again troubled by ice, but this time so thick that we could take long walks and exercise the dogs on it. The ship's wireless operator announced that on the night of our encounter with the iceberg four sealing ships had been lost, but their crews were safe, picked up by a fifth sealer. Our landing place, further north, was called Kangerdluksuak and here the climbing party, the Eskimos and dogs were put ashore, leaving the women and the archaeologists to occupy themselves searching for old Eskimo settlements and graves. I was shown, with great excitement, a necklace found in one of these and viewed with disillusionment a row of bits of walrus tusk.

After fifteen days away, August and the rest of the climbing party returned to the ship. They had reached the top of their desire and found it to be 12,250 feet high. It had been an intensely difficult climb, but they suffered nothing worse than snow blindness. So now, object achieved, it was time to turn for home. We departed on 30 August, under conditions of unearthly beauty. I quote from August's lecture to the Royal Geographical Society given the following year: 'During the day as the coastal mountains sank below the horizon, the Watkins range climbed up out of the sea until by evening we could make out all the high

20

tops. At sunset the lights were most beautiful. All the ice floes became a very pale rose while the water between them was the palest green and the sky behind was quite still with no sound. In the twilight, mirage changed the distant icebergs into all the fantastic shapes known to travellers in those parts.' The mountains also were miraged, so that one saw them quite literally standing on their heads. I have never seen the like before or since.

Our voyage home was calm and peaceful, and I remember our last night on board as we neared Aberdeen in idyllic conditions, leaning on the rail and watching the phosphorescent wake of the ship in the dark water. I had a feeling that we had returned from another world, not quite on this earth, but that I couldn't tell where the transition had taken place.

Years later, after August had died, I was very glad that the Danes named a glacier and a fjord, both at Kangerdluksuak, Courtauld's Glacier and Courtauld's Fjord, which names appear on the map of Greenland.

3

WARTIME

During the 1930s we divided our time between a small house in London, in Tite Street, and a farmhouse in Hampshire which August rented from Paul Latham, with whom he had been at school. The house of old red brick, standing in an exquisite garden, was by the Solent, only a short rough track dividing it from the water on which most of our days and sometimes nights were spent. I often wished more time could have been given to the garden. We sailed to the Channel Islands, rough and windy places, to Britanny and into Brest, venturing further down the Bay of Biscay. I have a sad memory of putting into some little French fishing port during a storm, where I saw what I took to be a fisherman's wife, shawl-clad, balancing herself against the wind on a cliff as she searched the stormy seas with anxious eyes. I had so often done the same – but *Duet* always came back.

Eventually we grew tired of two homes and in 1937 moved back to Essex, where August's roots were. We found a house three miles from the Suffolk border, and near enough to the rivers of Essex and Suffolk for *Duet* to anchor and make her sorties out to sea.

Our new home, Spencers, was a square white Georgian house built around 1760 by a descendant of the great Duke of Marlborough (hence its name from the Spencer-Churchill family). We painted the names of Marlborough's battles, Blenheim, Ramillies, Oudenarde and Malplaquet on our bedroom doors. The house stands in a small park with very fine trees and in those days a vociferous rookery, now alas departed, and the big Georgian windows let in much sunlight for the growing family.

Shortly after we had settled in, Henry Lamb came to paint a family portrait of Perina, Christopher and myself. I had wanted to postpone this since I was expecting my third child, but he protested that he liked painting pregnant women – they reminded him of his favourite Peter

22

Paul Rubens. He and I got on well together, and I liked his habit of
dashing to the piano between sittings – he stayed with us – and
pounding out something of J. S. Bach. He told me about his life with the
family of Augustus John, and I was suddenly reminded of Margaret
Kennedy's book *The Constant Nymph*, reputed to be written about the
John *galère*. I asked Henry Lamb if the character of Lewis Dodd in the
novel was drawn from himself. It was. Perhaps we got on too well
together since my husband referred to him irritably as 'that promis-
cuous little stoat', while Christopher, who, aged three, found it irksome
to sit still, called him 'the terrible Mr Lamb'.

Here at Spencers Julien, Stephen and William were born, the two last
during the Second World War. The first two years in this happy home
were shadowed by the coming storm; by the Munich crisis in 1938 and
then by the storm itself, which burst that morning of 3 September 1939.

Earlier that summer, in June, August had been asked to take *Duet* up
the coast of Norway, north from Bergen to Trondheim. I don't now
remember if the request came from the Foreign Office or the Admiralty,
but the idea was for owners of yachts to cruise the coasts of Europe from
western France to the north of Norway, apparently on holiday, but in
reality collecting as much evidence as they could of the size of piers,
capability of ports, positions of nearby factories and to collect picture
postcards of the areas, in readiness for the coming hostilities.

Duet sailed straight to Bergen, where I joined her, crossing the North
Sea in a Norwegian steamer. Our stretch of coast included some
forbidding fjords, from whose gloomy high cliffs and jagged mountain
tops squalls would come shrieking down to lay *Duet* on her side. I
remember one particularly fierce one when our skipper Bedford said, 'If
she'll stand this, she'll stand anything,' and I could well understand the
Norwegian myths of trolls living in these wild places. They seemed to
accord with the, to me, rather sad character of Norwegian art and
music.

I was not supposed to know the purpose of this particular cruise and
was much amused by the men putting their heads together and
whispering if they sighted a factory chimney, and nonchalantly 'pacing'
as they walked along the piers.

As we sailed further north the sun hardly set, and during the long
light nights the Norwegians would stand, lining the quay where *Duet*
lay, spitting, which seemed to be a national habit, on to her decks.

Michael Spender, brother of the poet Stephen, was with us and reacted angrily to the spittle directed at us as we slept below. He was a very dear friend who was killed flying during the last days of the ensuing war.

In a sunny interlude (most of this cruise was in dark, overcast weather) I remember going ashore at Andalsnes and seeing the stark word '*Krieg*' in a newspaper headline; it cast a shadow over that beautiful little harbour with thoughts of what lay ahead.

On our departure from the Norwegian coast a fog came down and stayed with us across the North Sea. August, with only one pale glimpse of the sun with which to fix our position, managed by his skill at navigation to steer *Duet* so that the next land we saw was the cliffside of Lerwick harbour in the Shetlands, for which he had been aiming.

September was a period of most exquisite autumn weather, with figs and peaches ripening on the walls, and none of us who had heard Neville Chamberlain's broadcast at eleven o'clock that morning of the 3rd will forget the hideous contrast between the harsh reality of his words and the peace and beauty with which England presented us that day.

August, who had joined the Royal Naval Volunteer Reserve, was recruited some months earlier into the secret service which later became SOE. I never discovered what he was up to in this hush-hush organization or where he went on their behalf, beyond that it was connected with explosives and that his journeys took him to the HQ in Baker Street and to a house in Hertfordshire.

On the outbreak of war he locked the billiard-room door and only the strange people who visited him were allowed inside. One of his visitors, Colonel Lawrence Grand, kept a pistol under his pillow, terrifying the housemaid who went to make his bed.

Before long August was called to the Admiralty, where he worked in Naval Intelligence in the famous Room 39. He was startled by the old-fashioned methods used by their lordships; when requesting a magnifying glass to study maps and charts he was told, 'Oh, we always use water bottles for that.' He was disgusted at being put in the Balkans Section when all his specialized knowledge was of Arctic waters. However, he was once summoned to the room of a high-ranking Admiral demanding to know if there was enough ice-free water for ships to pass to the north of Iceland . . .

While August fumed and fretted at being tied to a desk instead of being at sea, I, along with everyone else, listened with sick despair to the worsening news as the French were driven back and back after the German breakthrough at Sedan. On 14 June when the Germans entered Paris, André Maurois broadcast to us. He spoke, I remember, of the beauty of the morning, which seemed to make it all the more heartbreaking. I sat in our sunny rose-garden at Spencers and wept. (I was awaiting my fourth child, who was born two weeks later.) When our troops were being evacuated from Dunkirk, after the final fall of France, August's frustration boiled over. He longed to be taking *Duet* across to France with the armada of little ships bringing back the men from the beaches and, in Nicholas Wollaston's words, 'eventually, by displeasing his senior officers, he escaped.' He was sent to HMS *Hornet*, a shore establishment near Portsmouth, to train for command of a motor torpedo boat, known by the navy as MTBS. He decided that it would be a pleasant place for me to join him in a neighbouring house offering temporary accommodation for wives. Stephen, at six weeks old, could not be left behind, so he came too, with a nurse. He had been born on the festival of Saints Peter and Paul, and I had wanted to call him Paul after Paul Reynaud, who, at the head of the French Government, had refused to collaborate with the Germans when they overran France; August, however, insisted on a family name and Stephen he became.

Our arrival at Gosport coincided with the start of the Battle of Britain, and as I got out of the train carrying my baby, a frightened porter said, 'Get into that shelter, quick.' Everyone was running, while high, very high above us, tiny planes were wheeling amidst puffs of white smoke. I was witnessing the start of an historic and heroic battle, though I did not know it. The nurse, Stephen and I descended into the station shelter, where we sat amongst two rows of bewildered people facing each other on wooden benches in semi-darkness, and here I was forced to feed my poor child, overcome with guilt at having brought him into this situation. What strange ideas about the world he imbibed with his mother's milk we shall never know. Certainly they were not fears, since he grew up to be without them. Next day, leaving Stephen and the nurse in the comfortable country house August had found for us, I drove over to HMS *Hornet*, and here I was again hurried into a shelter, this time filled with Wrens, as Gosport was again being bombed. Amid all the noise one gun was particularly loud and I was told it was from August's MTB moored alongside where we were sheltering. When it was all over, he came down and joined us, wearing his tin helmet, and I was struck with the strangeness of our meeting underground after a six-week separation.

Stephen and I returned safely to the rest of the family at Spencers, where we had our own bombs. German planes not wishing to face the anti-aircraft barrage over London would drop their loads over the Essex countryside before going home, and there would be nightly thuddings round us while all the windows rattled and shook. There was no reason to think we might be hit, but with such random and haphazard bombing there was equally no reason to hope we might be missed.

On one occasion, when the warning siren was still a new horror, the household trooped down to the cellar (all except the three children, who were staying with my father- and mother-in-law while I waited for Stephen to be born). We had at that time an extremely proper parlourmaid, Jackson by name, who arrived prepared to meet the worst clutching her valuables. As the time went by, Jackson, who was sitting on a low stool, announced that it seemed to be getting damp and on inspection it was found that she was perched on an enormous round Stilton cheese which August had laid in as what he called 'iron rations' in case Essex was invaded by the Germans and we had to flee.

Another night, as I was lying in my bath, a bomb landed on the lawn and the window literally fell into the bathwater. And yet I think many people, looking back on those war years, would agree that they were strangely happy in spite of the anxieties, the partings, the losses and, in the towns, the horrors of bombardment. We were all united with one cause, one purpose, which gave us a satisfying sense of being bonded together in a common humanity. Also, in spite of the dangers, the quality of life seemed more solid, less fragile than it does today with the violence, racial hatred, hijackings and riots which are a commonplace now. Those nightly dronings of enemy planes overhead, with the consequent uncertainty of whether to let one's children sleep or move them downstairs; the voice of the announcer on the nine o'clock news saying, 'Some of our ships have been sunk'; these and others were intense anxieties at the time, but they were caused by a normal human reaction, whereas some of the violence and terrorism which we see almost nightly enacted on the TV screens nowadays belong to a nightmarish and incomprehensible world.

Very soon August suggested it would be safer for the children to sleep in the cellar below Spencers – at least they could go no lower – so I set about making it into an unconventional night nursery. It was barrel-shaped and surprisingly fresh and airy, and with carpet on the floor and four little camp beds, it was reasonably cosy. The children loved it, but their governess refused to share it with them until my bathroom bomb, which was in fact part of a stick which straddled the house, persuaded her down there.

It was very moving, during the nightly sessions with the nine o'clock news, as more and more countries of Europe became our allies, to hear the lengthening list of their national anthems. When our own was played, the children's governess, who sat beside the fire opposite me, would leap to her feet, eyeing me with distaste as I remained in my chair.

The village drains were not thought adequate to support an influx of evacuee children, so, instead, we had men from the local barrage balloon site billeted on us. They formed a welcome addition to our female society at Spencers. Occasionally large numbers of men and tanks would arrive and dispose themselves about the park, having camouflaged their tanks with branches from the trees. One charming commanding officer took the children for a ride, having announced, 'The children's tank is at the door.'

The war took me on many journeys around England and Scotland. August was sent from HMS *Hornet* with his MTB to Dover and there, during the bitter winter of 1940, I went to stay nearby. Dover was being shelled from across the Channel and I was allowed no nearer than the village of Eastry, where I stayed with three dear old ladies, friends of my mother-in-law, whose nineteenth-century way of life made them stipulate that when August came he smoked only in the smoking-room. Baths in that house were carried up to the bedrooms; ours, filled with tepid water, was placed before the bedroom fire.

When August was based at Ramsgate, I often stayed in an hotel there, listening at night with bated breath to the noise of bombardments out in the North Sea whenever I knew his ship was not in harbour. When visiting places on the coast, I needed an official pass which would be demanded at check points. Felixstowe was another place of brief and happy reunion, and so was Glasgow, where I travelled on the day that the first flying bomb arrived in England. It fell on the line somewhere near Liverpool Street Station, so disorganizing my train up from Essex that it became apparent I might miss my connection from King's Cross.

A helpful young airman told me he was also running late and planned to jump from the train as it was going slowly through the wasteland of Tottenham. He offered to help me out and, flinging open the train door, seized my luggage with one hand and my arm with the other. We landed safely on the platform and had the amazing good fortune to find a taxi, into which we both fell breathless. I just caught my train to Glasgow.

My experience of wartime Glasgow hotels was not a happy one. The place was full, but August had booked us a room in Sauchiehall Street, where the bathroom was of a squalor which sent me out to buy cleaning materials before I could get into the bath. At dinner we found a black feather (a rook's?) in our lobster, and there was a shrimp in our early morning teapot.

Yet these were but details, straws floating in the sea of our happiness at being together. Sheerness I have forgotten (the navy called it Sheer Nasty), but Rochester I will never forget. I had lately read *The Mystery of Edwin Drood* and this place, with its dark and brooding cathedral and the hotel where we stayed, full of Dickens' relics, seemed to breathe his spirit at every turn. The Dean of Rochester was living in the hotel – had he been bombed out of the snug, old red-brick house 'where Mr Dean directs his comely gaiters on finding himself not disagreeably reminded of his dinner'? This twentieth-century Dean could have stepped straight from Dickens' pages. Less Dickensian was an experience at dinner one night. There was a heavy raid on Rochester and, as the bombs whined down and the guns crashed up, the hotel staff and guests went from the dining-room to take shelter, leaving August and me solitary at our table. He continued calmly to eat his dinner, while I, petrified, had to pretend to do the same.

It was a wonderful change to travel up to Troon, where he had a ship building and where, from my hotel bed at night, I heard the soft waves lapping the shore, a nearly forgotten sound.

My mother and I took the three eldest children on a visit to Weymouth, where August was temporarily based, and heard in the train, to our great horror, that Weymouth had become a target town. Because of the blackout on all news about air raids, one took one's nearest and dearest in happy ignorance into the very eye of the enemy. During our days there, we were allowed limited access to the sandy beach, an almost unknown joy to wartime children, and with their father they happily built sandcastles, while at night-time my mother and

I agonized about taking them down to the hotel cellars. Twenty people were killed one night during our stay.

But in spite of all this, my trips to meet August provided a wonderful change from wartime Spencers, where life was routine-dull punctuated by acute anxiety.

Were were allowed only a gallon or two of petrol a month and I took to my bicycle or, while we still had a groom and a horse, drove about in our pony cart. (There had been much riding at Spencers in peacetime. August, who had hunted while at Cambridge, took it up again, he said, to please our old parlourmaid, who told him she liked looking after hunting clothes. He used to take Perina and Christopher on their ponies out with him, but I had never hunted and confined myself to riding side-saddle about the fields.) Pancake was fourteen hands and we were lucky to have kept her, Tanner the groom having made her stand in some dip in the yard to deceive the official who was requisitioning all horses of fourteen hands and over. Many things were requisitioned and it was taken for granted – land to be turned into food-producing fields, ash trees to provide wood for aircraft production, pots and pans if they were made of aluminium, and golden bibelots for some requirement I forget, though these last two were voluntary. One was made aware how little possessions mattered. Our old gardener refused to mow the lawns with only the cupful of petrol allowed for the motor mower, and the house gradually became surrounded by hayfields which August would scythe when home on leave. The food rationing was surprisingly good and, though we ate much less than in peacetime, we had enough and it was amusing making the weekly rations stretch as far as possible. However when milk was rationed, it became impossible to apportion it in a household of women, who to a large extent existed on, and whose happiness was determined by, cups of tea. I therefore decided to invest in two Jersey cows. I learnt the mysteries of buttermaking, sitting revolving a Kilner jar in my hands until the golden blobs in the milk turned into a solid lump. This was very satisfactory to me, but less so to the children, who disliked the taste. Another mystery I had to fathom was that of persuading a swarm of bees to go into their hive with the help of a white sheet spread on the ground and the moral support of my brave housemaid. It was certainly a wonderful moment when, safe behind my bee hat, I watched the gold and brown bodies going up the sheet and into their home.

A great happiness to me during some of these years was the companionship of my Napier uncle and aunt, who had left Italy when she entered the war beside Germany in 1940. They spent the summer in my aunt's old home in Cumberland, but came to me for the autumn and winter, and their presence filled me with comfort. My uncle, then in his sixties, would bicycle about the countryside collecting sheep's wool from the hedges and railings, which he would bring home in an old satchel. He had acquired an ancient spinning wheel and taught himself to spin, sitting peacefully treading the pedals for hours, while the soft wool turned itself into yarn under his hands and then into large untidy balls, from which my aunt would knit seaboot stockings for the navy.

The Napiers had no children of their own and adored mine; they could do no wrong. Aunt Dor, sitting down to tea, would say with a laugh, 'Chris has been sitting here – the chair's covered with honey.' They were ready to play any game, cards, 'Up Jenkins', whatever was popular, they would discuss anything that interested the children, enter any fun and provide much of their own. They were adored in return.

The children were a constant joy to me, for it was hard to be lonely with four growing minds keeping my attention with their intelligent questioning, helping my sanity with their matter-of-factness about the war (Julien, aged two, viewing the cellar and the racks of wine, said, 'What lovely bombs') and constantly surprising me with the difference a child sees in the world about it from the disillusion of the grown-up.

Nicholas Wollaston has described the camp that August organized for the children and myself at Pin Mill, a much loved place on the river Orwell in Suffolk, where we had often been sailing in peacetime. His flotilla was based in the river and he got permission from a farmer for tents to be pitched in his orchard by the waterside. We had a large bell tent for the three eldest children and for meals, and a small one for myself and August, when he could join me. Nanny, to her relief, had rooms for herself and Stephen in the village. It was cold, wet August weather when we arrived, but nothing dampened the younger spirits. Mine were slightly lowered at finding a large active wasps' nest in the floor of the bell tent, but August brushed aside my protests, promising that his sailors would come and 'take' it after dark. It was a happy carefree interlude, this short sojourn under canvas which, alas, has left no memories except of one night when we were invaded by August's sailors. He had arranged, for fun as well as for training, a combined exercise with the army, with a thousand soldiers being ferried over the river in whalers. Who were invaders and who the defenders I have forgotten, but I remember a party of sailors with blackened faces bursting through the trees and bushes of our camp and, to the delight of the children, volleys of bullets whizzing past our tents. I could only hope they were using blanks.

Next year, in 1943, our fourth son, William, was born. August was in the USA at the time, having crossed the Atlantic in the *Queen Mary* to help bring back a convoy of merchant ships. The Prime Minister was also a passenger in the *Queen Mary*, but August got no nearer to him than being put in charge of his boat. Mr Churchill never turned up for boat drill. The telegram which I sent to announce the new arrival included a list of suggested names and was returned by the censor: he thought it was in code.

And then, two years to the day from William's birth, on 8 May 1945, came VE Day and the ending of the war in Europe. A few weeks before I had written to August, 'I just can't get up the slightest enthusiasm over the end of the war. It's the most extraordinary thing how little it seems to mean, when the BBC gives out that Mussolini is chopped up and Hitler gone mad and Himmler wants to give in. And yet this time last year, if we could have heard these tidings, how joyful we'd have been.' We were all so tired, at such low ebb.

But when it actually happened one was caught up in the communal jubilation. I remember the sailors on Plymouth Hoe burning all the deck chairs in a frenzy of excitement. The Fire Brigade came, and they turned the hoses on the firemen. Lady Astor came to expostulate and they turned the hoses on her.

I went to a Plymouth church that day, where the congregation stood under open sky – the roof had been bombed and the aisles were covered with grass, and these reminders of what was now past filled our overflowing hearts with deep and fervent thankfulness. We wept unashamedly with joy.

4

PERILOUS SEAS

That autumn of 1945 August came home from the wars. I did not know it, but I was entering a decade of sadness with the serious illness of our son Christopher and the onset of August's terrible disease. But first it was all joy. And yet, behind the joy, I sensed, when the first weeks were over, that August was depressed. He was disillusioned and difficult to live with. I can give no better illustration of his state of mind than to cite his idea of being obliged to sell *Duet*. Only my tears of protest changed his mind; this conversation took place in the London Underground, a place so public that one does not weep there easily.

Many men and women returning after years of great responsibility and strain found it difficult to adjust to so-called peace. They had been stretched to their fullest, there was no longer the tension to keep them taut, but relaxation was not yet possible. August was no exception, for life with no particular occupation to return to made him extra vulnerable. True, he was elected to the Essex County Council, became a Deputy-Lieutenant and a JP and sat on many Committees including those of the National Association of Boys' Clubs and the Royal National Lifeboat Institution, but what were these compared with nearly five years almost continuously at sea?

The morale of the country was low. With the defeat of Winston Churchill's government at the war's end the Socialists had been elected, and their lack of experience was causing endless misery. Shortages were rife. Rations of food and clothing were reduced, even from wartime level, trains were cancelled since there was no coal to run them on, shops closed early because of the shortage of fuel for lighting and heating, and in any case there was very little for them to sell. It is difficult to convey the sense of contrast between what we had hoped the end of the war would bring and the bleak sense of privation in our lives.

Everywhere was austerity. When *Oklahoma!*, the ebullient musical comedy from America, was put on the London stage, the audience gasped at the women's clothes and the suede boots that the cowboys wore; it was an evening of glorious difference. I recall even as late as 1949, when August and I were in New York on our way to Jamaica, our amazement and slight disgust at the amount of bacon we were served for breakfast in our hotel: it was equivalent to more than a week's ration at home in one meal, and Rab Butler, as Chancellor of the Exchequer in the newly elected Conservative government, remembered stopping his car in the lanes of his constituency in 1951 to think deeply about ending the rationing of meat, which he decided to do – six years after the war was over.

But to return to that ending of the war, we, like our countrymen after the Treaty of Amiens in 1802, decided that with Europe once more open for travel, we would take our three oldest children abroad. It was not a wise decision. We went to Switzerland – to Champéry. The tickets, passports, etc., were all left to me, and so harassed must I have seemed that a woman on the cross-Channel steamer said it was brave of me to take four children abroad – she took August for my son. There were still mines at sea and the passengers were required to wear life-jackets, August inevitably refusing to co-operate in what he considered unnecessary fuss. The usual delectable dinner on the French train did not materialize and there was very little to eat, but I promised the children a glorious breakfast at the Swiss frontier, foolishly thinking back to those thick china cups of fragrant coffee and hot rolls of other years. Again we were disappointed.

The weather that summer was bad and the hotel not organized for children indoors. Nevertheless, August was determined to take us climbing; he had brought ropes and an ice-axe, and a guide was found to take us up one of the peaks in the Dent du Midi range. Great was the astonishment of other climbers at the hut, 8,000 feet up the mountain, to see Julien (8), Christopher (11) and Perina (12) eating their supper. Next day we started very early but, alas, there had been no clothing coupons for proper climbing equipment and August berated me for the fact that the children were not wearing climbing boots. I remember Julien manfully continuing to climb while sobbing with the cold. To my relief the guide said it was no longer safe, the bitter wind was blowing rocks off the mountain-side into our path and we must turn back. I was thankful. The next day, August, taking Christopher alone, set off on a higher peak, but a most violent thunderstorm came on, rattling and booming round the Alps, and caused them to lose their way. As the hours passed with no news of their return I became more and more anxious and consulted Madame at the hotel as to whether I should ask our guide of yesterday to look for them. Madame said, '*Monsieur est plus alpiniste que les alpinistes*,' and agreed that the guide should be sent. He was about to set off when, to my overwhelming relief, there was a telephone call from the mountain hut to say that they had arrived back, just as darkness fell.

It was a disastrous holiday, but next year, 1947, was worse. This was the summer of the outbreak of poliomyelitis and I remember thinking how lucky I was to move the entire family away from infection to a house on the west coast of Scotland. Mary Rennell, wife of Francis (he and his brothers, Peter and Taffy Rodd, were our lifelong friends) had recommended Shielbridge, a vast house near the mouth of Loch Shiel and the romantic Loch Moidart, which was to rent. It was the country of Bonnie Prince Charlie or the Pretender, whichever way you thought of him, and the seven trees commemorating the seven men of Moidart who followed his standard still stood at that Loch. August brought *Duet* to anchor in the bay by the ruined castle Tioram and we were joined by numerous friends and children. It was a very hot summer and everyone bathed, had picnics and sailed to their heart's content. I found an enormous plant of white heather by Loch Moidart, the only time in my life I have come across one; ever since then I cannot bear to see or touch white heather.

The plan when the holiday ended was for August and various friends to sail *Duet* back round the north of Scotland, taking Christopher and myself with him. I had the most powerful presentiment, the strongest feeling that Christopher should not come with us, but, though I pleaded, nothing would convince August that his twelve-year-old son should not accompany us, and we left at the beginning of September, just as the wonderful weather broke. I can hardly bear to write of that journey. We sailed round Cape Wrath, and forty-eight hours after departure were in Loch Eriboll, meaning to go ashore and visit John and Kat Buxton, holidaying nearby. Quite suddenly Chris and I were both stricken with sore throats so violent that I took our temperatures and found his to be 105° and mine 104°. We let the others go ashore without us. A small boat is not the place in which to be ill with anything more serious than seasickness, and, on reaching Thurso the next day, I insisted on seeing a doctor, who came on board and gave us drugs to bring down our temperatures. If only I had known the truth . . .

We sailed on into a nightmare. Christopher grew worse, with a headache that nothing would alleviate, the weather was really bad, and off that wild coast there was no help to be found and no one to turn to in my most cruel anxiety. Eventually we entered the River Tyne, flying a flag for a doctor, and to my utter despair he came aboard drunk. Finally we got our sick son into a nursing home in Newcastle, where, on his thirteenth birthday, as he was put into a proper bed after *Duet*'s cramped and hard bunk, he murmured, 'This is wonderful.' His illness was diagnosed as polio. When I telephoned Nanny, who had taken the other children home to Spencers by train, with the heartbreaking news, she told me that all four of them had developed the same terrible disease. They all made complete recoveries, but it took Christopher long years of brave struggle to regain his health. He had been going to Eton for the first time that autumn of 1947, but for many months he lay in plaster, continuing his education with a tutor.

Two years later he had a serious operation, a bone graft on his spine, from which he nearly died. The sister in his ward, who had become very attached to him, said she had never known anyone so ill to recover – but from the day after this operation, when we saw him, his face petal-white, with a tube up his nose and a drip into his arm, smiling from his bed, he climbed back to health. At Christmas that year, 1949, we set off for Jamaica, taking Perina with us, to complete his recovery. Ian Fleming, who had been with August at the Admiralty, offered to lend us his house, Goldeneye, where Christopher could swim in the warm tropical sea and learn to walk again. Much has been written about Goldeneye – for us the transformation from the cold of England's winter and all that we had gone through to this beautiful peaceful warm spot was unspeakably welcome.

Ian's cook-housekeeper, Violet, looked after all our wants. There were oranges growing in the garden, humming-birds among the flowers, and below the cliffs a few yards from the house a small private beach where we could swim inside the coral reef and, wearing rubber masks, float on our faces between the coral lagoons to find a weird and unbelievably wonderful fish-world. They were every colour, they were every shape, some even looked like owls.

At breakfast by Ian's enormous window we watched a man bobbing in his little boat at sea, catching the fish which Violet would cook for our lunch. We stayed in this tropical paradise for three months and while we were visiting a Jamaican doctor for the removal of an insect which had penetrated deep into my ear, I learnt the astonishing fact that I was to have another child. The birth of Susie, my sixth and last child, in August 1950, was the one really joyous event of those illness-saddened years, for in 1951 came the onset of August's illness.

We had our last happy holiday together that autumn of 1951. We took the car to Spain, driving down through France where the *vendange* was in full swing, and at every meal we enjoyed the small sweet white grapes which we saw piled on the bullock carts along the roads.

We drove through the Dordogne, where the country was wearing exquisite autumn colours, the hanging woods and the golden poplars by the wide quiet rivers reflecting the soft sunlight of October. We stayed at Périgueux, where the food in the Hotel du Domino was memorable beyond words; we visited the caves at Lascaux, open to the public in those days, and gazed spellbound at the mysterious and marvellous wall-paintings of animals, bulls, horned creatures and ponies with stiff erect ruffs, which were shown to us by torchlight since electricity had not yet been installed.

When we reached Arcachon, August felt impelled to bathe in the Bay of Biscay and bought himself a pair of swimming trunks. It was a cold October evening, but he insisted that he had enjoyed the water. Later, when he became ill, I wondered if it was from a chill. . . .

Entering Spain at San Sebastian one immediately felt the enormous contrast from the Basque country through which we had come. There was *gravitas*. One saw it in the handsome police with their shiny black theatrical headwear; even the nursemaids in their lace aprons pushing elaborate prams along the sea-front had a charming dignity.

Then to Burgos, driving along one of the sacred pilgrim routes running from France to Santiago de Compostella. It was late when we arrived and we made straight for the cathedral before it shut. I remember the sense of awe conveyed by its dark Gothicness, its space, the towering pillars, and the silver gleaming on the many altars through the little remaining light of that late October evening. Next day, visiting the monastery of Las Huelgas, my imagination was fired on seeing the tomb of a little English princess Eleanor, daughter of a King of

England, who had come to this windswept corner of Spain in the twelfth century to marry Alphonso VIII, King of Castile. What were communications like in those days, I wondered. Did the pilgrims bring her news from home? She probably knew not a word of Spanish, and died far from her native England. Some material from her dresses were preserved in the monastery, stretched behind glass, the finest woven linen and wool thread which, I was glad to see, was lined with fur, since the stimulating air of Castile is cold.

To reach Madrid we crossed the striking Sierra de Guadarrama. Everything in Spain seemed striking, with strong contrasts, from the bold rocks and deep shadows of the Sierra, to the paintings of the Spanish School in the Prado. Here the works of Goya, Zurbarán and Ribera are instantly recognizable, with their fierce faces and sharply defined colours, from the more gentle Italian and French Masters in that wonderful gallery. There is a *Descent from the Cross* by Roger van der Weyden, which for me transcends everything else in the Prado. The utter deadness of the Christ and the collapse at his feet of the stricken Mary are intensely moving.

Our arrival in Madrid had been somewhat of a nightmare. The Ritz Hotel had not confirmed August's booking of a room, and it appeared that none was available. There followed a frantic search when we crossed and recrossed the streets of Madrid, only possible when a policeman blew his whistle, to find all the other hotels equally full. In despair we returned to the Ritz to plead with the hall porter, when August tried name-dropping. 'Oh, if you have an introduction to the Duke of Alba I can certainly fit you in,' was his response!

In those days the wines of Spain, at least in the villages, were perhaps rougher than they are today. Certainly on our way to visit the monastery of Escorial, I felt my head drumming with the white wine we had drunk, lunching at a small wayside café. As we drove up to this vast and imposing building I remember putting my head on August's shoulder, murmuring as I did so, 'Too big – drive on.' (I was to correct this omission years later.)

The road to Toledo was, in those days, a sandy dirt one along which camels daintily picked their way and laden donkeys trotted. The city presents itself, more than three hundred years after El Greco painted it, amazingly faithful to its portrait which is in the Metropolitan Museum in New York. Neither of us had experienced the works of El Greco face

37

to face before and the *Death of the Count of Orgaz* was a revelation before which we sat speechless.

But already, even that day in Toledo, August felt ill and we went back early to Madrid. He was attacked by a strange virus which, subsiding, left him subtly changed, so that after we returned home life was never quite the same again.

My father had died earlier that year, and I relate this because it was the only occasion when I ever knew August to shed tears, whereas when his mother died the following year he demonstrated this new strangeness by reading the Lesson at her funeral wearing a bright scarlet waistcoat that Perina had given him. He joined the Royal Yacht Squadron and wore their uniform, he who had always mocked the smart side of sailing. I found it bewildering. In 1953 Christopher, by this time at Eton, had been chosen to sail in the school team against other schools on the Holy Loch, near Glasgow. August offered to sail him and the rest of the crew to Scotland in *Duet*, but my heart sank when he telephoned me from the Wash, to say he did not think he could go on – he wasn't feeling up to it. He *did* go on, but I was wild with anxiety: what was wrong with August, of all people, not to want to be sailing? I was soon to know.

The first clinical signs came that autumn of 1953 when his eyesight started to go; I vividly remember his telling me, after dinner in our drawing-room, that during that day in London he had found he couldn't see out of one eye. I instantly went up to my bedroom, put on a coat and told him that, late as it was, we were going to our local doctor, who then and there made an appointment with an oculist in Cambridge. Before seeing him, there came a terrible day when, shooting with our old friends, Nigel and Nancy Capel Cure, August couldn't see the birds at all. He had always been one of the best shots in Essex, and the Capel Cures' keeper was almost as distressed as I was. The prognosis of the oculist was not hopeful, and then it was that a neurologist told me, but not August, that he had multiple sclerosis. I was ignorant of its terrible meaning, but Francis Rennell, our ever-faithful friend, revealed to me what I might have to expect. It seemed to me that my life was at an end.

I was August's eyes that winter, reading to him, writing his letters and walking him arm-in-arm about the lanes and fields. When he had a remission, when his eyesight improved, he was wonderfully brave, trying to live life normally and ignoring the various symptoms which beset him. But inexorably the evil illness took a hold, reaching out to all parts of his body and finally his brain, so that by 1954 I knew that my most dear and loved husband had left me as the person I knew to be gradually superseded by a stranger . . .

This tragic situation is best described by Nicholas Wollaston who, though he never knew August, writes most poignantly in the last chapter of *The Man on the Ice Cap*:

That ordinary chap – 'the normal man' whose voice had come up the ventilator pipe at the ice-cap station and who had been hoisted by his friends through the roof of the tent into the bright spring morning – was attacked more than twenty years later by an enemy against whose terrors, unlike those of solitude or a snow-quake, he had no defence. A form of multiple sclerosis was diagnosed in 1953, when he was forty-nine. His courage and quiet cheerfulness, though he never surrendered them, were useless in a losing battle that lasted nearly six years . . . Such was the agony of August's last years. His eyes, his limbs, his brain were destroyed in turn as if by the creeping cold that had failed before.

He died after a world of suffering to himself and his family, on 3 March 1959, aged only fifty-four years, and was buried at sea as he had requested.

But during those years when, torn with pity, I often wished for death myself, I was given a miracle. It seems heartless to write thus, but it was the truth. In 1954 Rab Butler's wife Sydney had died of a very distressing form of cancer, leaving him bereft and lonely. He and I turned towards each other for mutual comfort, and in doing so found a depth of devotion which was to last for the rest of our lives. Much is written about young love, but love in middle life is like a renaissance and is as strong as anything I have ever known. I was able to stand the anguish of my life at home during those years because of the support given me by Rab.

5

MAGIC CASEMENTS

There were some who thought our marriage on 21 October 1959 was too soon: they did not know how long ago August had left me.

Rab had warned me that the moment we announced our engagement I should be besieged by the press. Even so I was not prepared for the dramatic suddenness with which this took place. The announcer on the nine o'clock news had ended his bulletin with the fact that the Home Secretary was to marry again, and his voice was scarcely off the air when the front door bell was violently rung. The attack had begun and the gentlemen of the press, soon to become my friends, were outside.

We decided on a quiet wedding in a beautiful church in the village of Ashwell, which was near enough to both our homes to be convenient, and where Perina lived. She was to give a party afterwards for the two families, his and mine, but we had not reckoned on the press. In their devious way they discovered our plans, telephoning someone at Eton to find out when my son William was getting a night off, and the result was there were more press and police present than wedding guests. Hubert Ashton, Rab's PPS, who was also his best man, kept up a running cry, 'Perina, we must have more champagne for the police,' who had come in hordes to see the Home Secretary safely married. The drive on to the tarmac at Heathrow and the flight to Rome in two seats discreetly reserved in the front of the first class of the plane, passed in a dream, as did our honeymoon in Rome, limited to five days because Rab had to get back for the opening of Parliament.

I had forgotten such happiness existed as that to which I was raised by my marriage to Rab. I was raised in many ways, but the happiness was the most important. His quiet consideration for me, ('I'll look after you, Pussy,') was a new experience; I had never been cared for in that way before, and to be the object of care by so great a man filled me with wonder. But his consideration for people stretched far beyond me; it was one of his most prominent characteristics, for which he was greatly loved, particularly by the humble who had no reason to fear his intellect as they were not made aware of it.

I approach writing about Rab with extreme discretion, a mixture of delicacy and caution. How can I write about this distinguished statesman? A very perceptive Fellow of Trinity College said, years later, in a broadcast about him, that he was reminded by Rab of a kaleidoscope: there were so many bits. This is what is daunting. An orator, a philosopher, an amateur painter, an intellectual, a humourist, a Christian, a countryman, a lover of literature – the list is endless. But it is not by listing his qualities that one can portray the man. Rab was all these, and many more rare and lovely attributes fitted unto his personality. The two words which for me best describe him are '*bonté*' and 'nobility'. I use the French word because, compared with the equally lovely word 'goodness', I feel it has a warmer, more benevolent meaning which was closer to Rab's outlook on life, and nobility was as natural to him as breathing. He was incapable of an ignoble thought or action. I may be thought, like Lear, foolish and fond, but I am not alone in believing he was a uniquely great human being. He constantly made me laugh: I have never met anyone with whom it was so consistently amusing to be. It is frustrating not to be able to reproduce this light-hearted, happy atmosphere; his company was like a fire on a bitter night which both glowed and sparkled. No wonder I was happy.

He used to pay me a very strange compliment: 'I want to be buried with you.' It seemed to me the ultimate accolade.

He had a charming way of rebuking me: 'Think of others, Pussy,' (or 'Growler', my alternative name), if he wanted another cup of tea; and if the rebuke was more serious, such as, 'I didn't want to talk to so-and-so, why did you make me?' he would run his words together and speak in an assumed voice, as though pretending to correct me. I never heard a man with such a beautiful speaking voice. It was not only what he said, but the sound of him saying it that held one.

Long before I loved him I remember a political meeting in our village before an election, when the postmistress said to me, 'I could listen to Mr Butler for ever.' But it was not his voice alone which cast a spell. From the moment that he rose to speak, in Parliament or on a platform, he seemed to give out a mysterious force. He had (that overworked word) 'charisma'.

Norman St John-Stevas, when he was writing for the *Economist*, said to me at a Conservative Party Conference, 'You are wonderful when your husband is speaking; you look so rapt.' It was quite simply that I was rapt. Rab was a mysterious man in that the contrasts in his character covered such a wide range – on the one hand the civilized, well-informed, sophisticated, worldly politician, and on the other someone capable of almost childish behaviour. He once telephoned me from Crewe railway station where his train was waiting and I asked him how he had got rid of his detective.

'Oh,' replied Rab, 'he can't see me – I've taken the lightbulb out of the telephone box.'

He was adorably unconcerned about his appearance, yet somehow managed always to appear *tiré à quatre épingles*. He often concealed in his trouser pocket a bottle of wine to be produced at the right moment without in the least damaging his silhouette. A less attractive habit was the concealment of food in his pocket since he was unable to leave anything uneaten on his plate and preferred to hide it. Once, after a Lord Mayor's banquet, he gave me a highly scented note; it had spent the evening nestling beside a piece of salmon. We were staying on one occasion at a house in Yorkshire where the Queen Mother was also a guest. Rab packed for the visit himself and on arrival I was mortified to see a footman laying out his evening shirt, frayed at both cuffs and collar. When worn by Rab, such was his presence, the shirt went unnoticed. It was this presence which was also mysterious: I have not met it in many, but it is unmistakable when there and captivating when allied to sweetness of nature and goodness of heart.

> Tell me where is fancy bred,
> Or in the heart or in the head?
> How begot, how nourished?

could be said equally of this attribute.

He was very attractive to women. Philip Ziegler, in his biography of Lady Diana Cooper, writes: 'Lady Waverley wanted her to marry R. A. Butler, which Diana interpreted as a sure sign that she had her eye on him herself.' A certain London hostess had also wished to marry him: 'I hear he's found a little woman from the provinces,' she announced. Rab was delighted with this remark when it was repeated to us. 'Madame Bovary' he cried!' 'I shall call you Emma Bovary.'

"IF RAB BUTLER CAN TAKE ON TEN KIDS AND TWO JOBS', SHE SAID, 'SURELY YOU CAN COPE WITH ONE OF EACH.'"
— DAILY SKETCH 17/10/57

Again I marvelled at the providence which had led me to his side. Perhaps the ambivalence of his nature, the sophisticated and the child-like, appealed equally to a woman's sense of glamour and her maternal instinct. But these are all the small change of a loving partnership which grew over the years. I was to learn each week more about the man I had married. Bob Menzies, when Prime Minister of Australia, said, 'Rab is the wisest man in the world', and years later our Dean at Trinity College, Harry Williams, said of him that he obeyed Our Lord's instruction, 'Be ye as wise as serpents.' He was, above all, a pragmatist and thereby saved himself much anxiety and turmoil. When, as Chancellor of the Exchequer, he said that the balance of payments situation was as though England's life-blood was draining away, I asked him how he could bear to live with such a fact. He replied, 'You can't take it to bed with you and survive.' He applied the philosophy of his book *The Art of the Possible* to every problem in private and public life. But his wisdom in public life was not always profited from and therein lay a great waste.

It was not perhaps understood by some that occasional whimsicality and frivolity of manner hid the most formidable intellect. Just as he never bothered about his clothes or appearance, so he didn't trouble too much about what people thought of him – not from arrogance, but from intelligence 'I know I mean this or that, others will realize it also.' However elliptically said, he assumed an intelligence equal to his own which would understand.

If he didn't bother with his own clothes he was particular about mine, with a very good eye for what was chic and what was not. He was fastidious in his ideas about women; they must not yawn, it was ugly, and they must never, never have a second helping of food. He was gloriously unaware of his surroundings. We were once lunching in a tiny restaurant on the harbour of Beaulieu, in the South of France. Rab's bad hand made it difficult for him to eat spaghetti in the normal way, since he couldn't twist his fork to lift the strands to his mouth, so he would scoop it up all anyhow. I can see now the look of astonished disbelief on the face of the Frenchwoman at the next table as Rab hauled down the strings of pasta which descended from his mouth, rather like a seaman handling ropes, to rescue them for another forkful.

He proceeded with great caution. Before we were married he invited me to a luncheon at 11 Downing Street consisting of Commonwealth Prime Ministers. Afterwards I enquired why. 'I wanted to see how you would swim in those waters,' he replied.

So I flew back with him from Rome that October day to test the new waters. Our first party together was formidable: it was an evening reception at Admiralty House given by the Prime Minister. The moment we arrived Rab was snatched away to an inner room by Harold Macmillan and I was left, it seemed, with the whole of London gazing at the Home Secretary's new wife. Mercifully I saw someone I knew and the ice was broken. Our next engagement was warmer. It was the Lord Mayor's Banquet, where Rab and I got a tremendous reception. During the evening the TV cameras showed the nation the Home Secretary's new wife quite often, I was told by my mother, who, no doubt from the kindest motives managed to criticize my careful coiffeur and behaviour generally. 'Should you have talked so much to Rab and not to your other neighbour?' My other neighbour was M. Chauvel, the French Ambassador, whose faultless English came shooting out with the speed of a machine-gun. Ted Heath was once forced to implore him to speak more slowly, saying, 'My English cannot keep up with yours.'

This tremendous change in my life had brought me four step-children. Richard and Adam, the two eldest sons, were both married and living away from home, but James was up at Cambridge, where he and my son Julien attended lectures together. He may not have relished the invasion of his home by so many stepbrothers and sisters, plus two horses, three dogs and Susie's guinea-pigs. He told the Master's wife at Pembroke, his College, that he was off home to stake a claim to his room. In later life, however, we became and have remained devoted friends who confide freely in each other. And then there was Sarah – her mother Sydney had asked me before she died to look after her. Sydney seemed to have had a strange prescience about the future. She wrote to Rab's elder sister, Iris Portal, that Rab would marry me when he was left, an extraordinary prophecy, since he and I were not close at the time of her death.

I tried to look after the motherless Sarah and was rewarded by a great welcome when I became her stepmother. She was open, confiding, amusing and clever, and we formed a happy relationship. When she went to McGill University in Canada, she wrote on her entry form that she had seven brothers so wholly did she accept her four stepbrothers, equally taking under her wing the much younger Susie.

Some of my own children had left home. Perina was married; Christopher had come down from Trinity and was at Westcott House training for the priesthood; and Julien, who during my saddest winter had regularly motored six hours in a Land-Rover from Catterick, where he was doing his National Service, to visit me at weekends, had followed Christopher to Trinity. Stephen was abroad learning French and William was still at school. They all accepted their new home philosophically, and their stepfather with joy.

Rab had been made Chairman of the Conservative Party on the day we announced our engagement. He was already leader of the House of Commons, and all this, as well as his duties as Home Secretary, made for an intensely full, demanding and busy life. As Chairman's wife, I was constantly invited to speak at bazaars, fêtes and gatherings all over the country. Fortunately I did not mind speaking as long as I had something to say, and I had luckily had quite a lot of experience, although only on a county level. My first engagement was amusing. It was to open a Christmas bazaar somewhere near London and I was sent by car with a charming MP who was also my 'minder'; Central Office must be reassured that the Home Secretary's wife was 'safe'. I was provided with a speech which I tore up in the car, saying I preferred to make my own. The 'minder' hid his fears with great gallantry and in the event all went well. After that I was sent from Carlisle to Cardiff, and even Scotland, and enjoyed meeting the people who welcomed me, but of course the greatest pleasure was to accompany Rab when he had a speaking engagement: the thrill of hearing him speak was never to leave me.

It was wonderful, in the House of Commons, where I became a regular in the Speaker's Gallery, to see how, when Rab rose, the empty seats would fill. I found the House of Commons endlessly interesting: the mysteries of procedure, the moments when Rab would get up from the front bench to loll over the box where his advisers sat just beyond the Speaker's chair, the intricacies of voting, in which the Speaker's wife and I agreed that some members seemed simply to follow each other without knowing which lobby they were going to – no doubt we were guilty of a sort of *lèse-majesté*. I came to know the various policemen and the exquisitely courteous ushers in their evening tails, with gold plaques gleaming against their starched shirt-fronts. It was an enormous advantage to be Rab's wife in that place; he was so popular (I am not now referring to the extreme right-wing back-benchers) that some of the popularity spilled over on to me.

At weekends we would go home to Essex, where his house, Stanstead Hall, was only ten miles from Spencers, and there would be more speaking engagements in the villages of his enormous constituency, Saffron Walden. He often brought the following story into his speeches. 'I am reminded of the old Frenchman who was asked what was the secret of his long and happy marriage. The reply was: "On our marriage we decided that my wife would settle all the minor decisions and the major ones would be left to me." "Well, then?" "No major decisions have ever arisen!" '

On other weekends there might be a shoot. Rab was very fond of shooting and, on his day, very accurate. An accident as a child had left him with a slightly disabled right arm, but his guns had been built to accommodate this. He loved the whole scene – the beaters, the dogs, and the days out in the Essex air and the country he knew so well. A faithful friend who came every season to shoot with him was Michael Adeane, the Queen's Secretary, bringing his wife Helen. They were great favourites.

There were, of course, trials for me. The staff at Stanstead had enjoyed nearly five years without a mistress in the house and were determined to show their resentment at my arrival, but I refused to occupy the position of the heroine in *Rebecca*, Daphne du Maurier's novel, and eventually the waters grew calm. I had an ally in Fred Smith. He had been Rab and Sydney's groom and had shown much understanding of Rab's dislike of horses during his disastrous and short-lived attempt at hunting.

On one occasion, out with the hounds, his mount ran away with him. Rab's damaged hand made controlling the animal difficult, but with great skill he steered it into a thorn bush, where the prickles brought it to a standstill. Rab was then able to dismount and lead it home. Horses were the only animals I ever knew Rab not to love.

Fred was now Rab's chauffeur and close confidant, passing on all the gossip of the neighbourhood and constituency. If Rab had ever given me any reason to be jealous, it would have been of the much-loved Fred.

There would be guests at weekends – Rab's dearest friends Freddy and Sheila Birkenhead, who also became mine, his sister Dor Middleton and her husband Laurence, Philip and Mollie Swinton. Philip was wonderful with young people and took a great fancy to Julien, while she called herself 'Inferior Mollie' in mock deference to me. Their home in Yorkshire was one of the few places where Rab allowed us a visit at a weekend, to shoot grouse. I use the word 'allowed' because weekends were usually sacred to Stanstead and the affairs of his constituency, which he loved to call 'the granary of England'. He had a quick eye for natural beauty and we rejoiced in our mutual love of the countryside, the seasons and what they brought.

Another great relaxation was his painting. His interest had been fired by Winston Churchill, and he tells the story in *The Art of the Possible* of a combined attempt – Sir Winston of the sea and Rab of the mountains – in the South of France when Sir Winston grew jealous of Rab's efforts. He learnt much from lessons with Edward Seago, shared by Lord

Alexander, in Norfolk; Rab considered Alex the best amateur painter he knew. I had also had lessons when a child and had learnt the laws of perspective, something unknown to Rab, so that when we visited Venice together I was able to point out that the roof of the Dogana, which he was painting from the balcony of our hotel across the Grand Canal, went up and not down as he had drawn it. I do not think he ever quite believed me, though I tried to demonstrate, as I had been taught, with a piece of string.

Our visit to Venice in 1960 was a revelation to him. He went about, face and trousers smeared with paint, totally immersed in the city's beauty, and it was delightful to see him welcomed by the hall porter at our hotel as '*Eccellenza*' on returning home from a painting morning in this state. He was captivated by Venice and I was deeply happy to revisit all the remembered places and pictures with him. The Consul lent us his launch for trips to the Lido and there was a moment of comic horror when Rab decided the bathing huts out there were too expensive and he would change into his bathing trunks in the cabin of the launch. On they went with ease but, getting dressed again over them for a suitable arrival, his trousers refused to go over the shoes which he had omitted to take off. As the launch sped swiftly towards the landing stage, Her Majesty's Home Secretary was struggling madly to get back into his trousers, while I, choking with laughter, could only just get out, '*Più piano per piacere*,' to our driver. As Nanny once said, 'You never know what will happen when you go out with Mr Butler,' though she was referring to nothing more dramatic than a walk in the Essex woods. Nanny was wonderful in continuing her imperturbable life in the nurseries at Stanstead in exactly the same fashion as she had done at Spencers, jealously guarding her rights at nursery tea, to which the whole party came, and bringing out the age-old nannyisms, '*She's* no oil painting', 'Who's going to look at *you*, dear?' etc.

If I have forgotten much of these happy, busy first years with Rab, perhaps it is because they were so full, so crowded with engagements both in London and the country that memory has become overloaded and spilled some of its cargo. I was naturally enormously proud to be his wife and to go about with him on great and small occasions and, looking back as I do now I am alone, everything of those days seems to be covered with a sort of radiance. He used often to quote to me Ronsard:

Quand vous serez bien vieille, au soir à la chandelle
Assise auprès du feu, devisant et filant
Direz, chantant mes vers, en vous esmerveillant:
Ronsard me celebroit du temps que j'estois belle.

6

HEBRIDES OVERTURE

Our attachment to Mull, off the west coast of Scotland, started in 1960 when Rab's PPS James Ramsden suggested we might lease Knock from Lord Masserene. I was familiar with the island from sailing on that coast with August, and pressed the idea, and so started our 'endless adventure'.

Knock was a typical Scottish lodge standing at the head of Loch na Keal, a deep dark loch in which it was said part of the British navy had sheltered during the First World War. Ben More, the highest mountain on the island, frowned down upon it and brought incessant rain. The beds were damp, the curtains and carpets were damp and, there being no drying-room, a pulley was fixed on the kitchen ceiling for wet garments, which dripped on to the table below. It was the most uncomfortable house I have ever stayed in. However, nothing daunted the spirits of the large party which descended upon it with Rab and me. A certain number of bedrooms had been advertised, but it was found that they did not quite tally with those existing, and some doubling up was necessary. Nanny's bed collapsed regularly and Rab's wonderful detective as regularly mended it. We had eight or nine adult guests and as many children, so housekeeping was no sinecure, but it was made easy by Mr and Mrs Macphail who ran the place – he as stalker and she as cook, and both equally charming. The fishing ghillie ran away on the first day of our holiday, but we had plenty of boys to man the boats without him. The fishing and stalking were wonderful for those who enjoyed them. Rab sometimes went with the stalkers, but came more often with the children and me for bathing-picnics (he was extremely fond of swimming), when he would also set up his easel and paint. He won ten-year-old Susie's heart by christening a bridge where the cattle liked to congregate 'Big-Job Bridge'.

On one occasion we paid a visit to Iona. Rab had hired the Iona ferry boat to pick us up from the Island of Inch Kenneth, near the mouth of Loch na Keal, which belonged in those days to Lady Redesdale. I don't think we planned the impertinence of landing on her island, but merely to transfer our large party from our unseaworthy Knock boats into the sturdy ferry boat off its shores. In the event our boats, unreliable as always, broke down and we were landed in relays and in pouring rain on to the sodden shingle beach, where Rab, directing operations from a little lump of wet rock, ordered lunch to proceed. Lady Redesdale, viewing these castaways on her island, sent a maid to invite us into her house, but we regretfully declined, being too wet and too numerous.

Iona itself was disappointing. I had visited it nearly thirty years earlier, with almost no one on the island in those days and the cathedral a ruin, but the whole place echoing with its past. Now it was loud with tourists and with souvenir shops. A young man insisted on 'explaining' the cathedral, though it transpired he had arrived from the south only twenty-four hours earlier. A lady in a grocer's shop refused to sell me the number of slabs of plain chocolate I asked for, saying that I could not possibly want so much; she was evidently fed up with the invading hordes, including ourselves. The best part of the expedition was the crossing in the ferry boat which brought us all the way back to Knock – a large sturdy boat made of vast timbers resembling the vessels which illustrate medieval manuscripts.

We discovered beautiful empty white sandy beaches to the north of Mull, where, the hills being lower, it rained less. Jean and Niall Rankin invited us to lunch at Treshnish House near Calgary, and Rab and I determined to find a house of our own in that part of the island, which seemed to us more *riant* and less frowned on by mountains.

This we did in January 1961, when we travelled to Mull specially to look at Frachadil. I shall never forget my first sight of it, on a day of brilliant winter sunshine, perfectly still, with not a cloud in the bluest sky and everywhere the bracken turned to gold. I knew as soon as I saw it that it was to be ours. I loved its plain, uncompromising white stone face looking nearly due north to the islands of Rhum, Eigg and Skye, all bold and visible that day, even to the snow on the Cuillin mountains of Skye, although we were to find the islands often hid themselves in rain or mist. The house stood on the side of a hill, surrounded by nine acres of rough moorland and grass. There was a walled garden running down to the Frachadil burn, but this was a wilderness and was to remain so, as

51

everything we planted was eaten by sheep. Inside the house were long passages and winding shallow stairs, off which were many tiny bedrooms. It was simple and plain with nothing to jar the senses or prevent the cosiness, comfort and warmth which I planned. It was the only investment that I have ever made and it was totally successful. Rab and I spent twenty summers there and very often went up in winter and at Easter, in fact so much did he love it that my occasional suggestion of a holiday in France or Italy generally went unheeded. It is difficult to convey in words the magic of that place; its hold upon our hearts was absolute.

The number of rooms meant that we could have large parties of both our families to stay and they mostly became as enthusiastic about everything as we were. We bought a boat, a twenty-one foot open diesel launch which Susie, who was a keen ornithologist in those days, christened *Gannet*, and she lay in Calgary Bay, a mile and a half from the house. Calgary has at least two claims to fame. From this tiny hamlet of not more than a dozen crofts, went out an intrepid Scotsman to found the North West Canadian Mounted Police and to name their new home, Calgary; and in the post office, probably the smallest in the British Isles, lived the family of McQuarie, descended from that very McQuarie after whom the river in New South Wales is called and also McQuarie Island in the Australian Antarctic Sea.

Rab found a boatman in Tobermory for the *Gannet*. He was a great character named Callum Robertson, who had been a sailor on board MacBrayne's steamers, but, more importantly for us, had spent his summers when a young man with his fisherman father on the uninhabited Treshnish Islands and was intimate with all the rocks and shoals in the water round Mull.

For our first outing he took us on a day of bright sun and strong wind across eleven miles of open sea to the island of Coll. It will be remembered that Dr Johnson on his journey to the Western Isles crossed to Coll in very bad weather when James Boswell, terrified, was only soothed by being given a rope to hold. Our little boat bounced over the waves, causing Nanny, sitting under the hood up in the bows, to look a trifle worried, but Callum assured her all was well. However, afterwards we discovered that Callum's daughter was staying on Coll and he wished to show off his new command.

We went many times to the Treshnish Islands with Callum, nosing through the islands and observed only by round-eyed seals lying basking on the rocks, who would glide into the water at our approach and swim nearer to the boat to satisfy their curiosity. Unmeasured was the joy of slipping into these waters oneself and, pushing away from the sucking seaweed, take to the 'glassy cool translucent wave' – never were there cleaner, clearer, more inviting seas to swim in.

But to return to *Gannet*, there were many rocks between the islands and, as all eyes were overboard searching for them in the narrow channels, the boys treasured Rab's saying, 'In my profession we are taught to keep away from the rocks.' On one occasion we landed on Lunga, the biggest island of the group, to see the thousands of kittiwakes nesting on the Harp Rock. As we went ashore Callum called out, 'Don't be long. When the tide turns, we shall have a fine smash of sea with wind against tide.' On shore it was hot, and Rab, lying in the sun watching the *King George*, a vast Victorian-looking vessel which took daily trips round the Inner and Outer Hebrides, murmured how absurd it was of Callum 'to worry about the tide – look how steady the *King George* is.' However, we did indeed have a smash of sea before we got clear of the islands. Fortunately we had Julien with us to control the throttle when the big waves hit us as Callum steered us through to open water.

After a year or so Callum left us: he married a strong-minded widow who carried him off to a shore life in Lytham St Anne's. This blow was softened by his brother Johnny coming to look after the *Gannet*, but Johnny was deaf and his eyesight was not good. ('Will that be a buoy or a fishing smack over yon?') and it was decided that the boat must be moved to Tobermory for his greater convenience, as he lived there.

This was far less amusing since Tobermory harbour opened into the Sound of Mull and one was obliged to go east, to the dark and claustrophobic mainland or up and down the Sound itself rather than out to sea. Christopher was for some years chaplain at the London Hospital and on his holidays he would bring *Duet* to Mull with a crew of doctors and anchor her in Tobermory harbour, greatly to Johnny's admiration.

Sometimes *Duet* would approach us from the west and I had the extraordinary experience of talking to Christopher on his ship-to-shore radio while watching him sailing off the shores visible from the windows of Frachadil. Johnny always called Christopher 'the Major' for some unexplained reason, while Rab was 'the Lord'. Tourists enquiring if *Gannet* was for hire would be startled by his reply, 'Ye'll need to ask the Lord.' When Johnny eventually retired, we brought the boat round to Loch Tuah on the west coast, to a tiny harbour called Port na Criche, which had been used years ago for coal to be delivered to Mull by steamer, before the roads were made. This delicious place, with its tumble-down pier and slippery rocks, on which we came ashore, was to remain the *Gannet*'s permanent home, from where with the aid of Rab's Scottish cousins, the Corsar family, who had followed us to Mull, we would sally once more out to the open sea, across to Gometra, Ulva and beyond.

The routine in Mull was very relaxed. Most people came down to breakfast in dressing-gowns and a discussion would then be held on plans for the day. Lunch was always a picnic, on wet days round the living-room fire and, if fine, on the hill, the beach or the boat. I had inherited with the house a very decrepit grand piano; there was no tuner on the island and most of its strings were broken, so I was quite glad when it was requested as a gift for a local village hall, but Rab was dismayed. 'On what are we going to carve the ham at lunch time?' he asked.

Rab leased 30,000 acres of rough stalking from Eddie Compton of Torloisk and, though he never shot a stag himself, he and I would enjoy walks of unparalleled beauty with Roddy MacCrae, his stalker, and whoever else was after the stag, up to where they were to be found, stopping on the way to spy. Spying was indeed what we were doing on these secret delicate creatures who, hidden against the hill to the naked eye, were discovered by Roddy's telescope and then by our non-professional binoculars as they fed or lay at their ease. Lunch, very light, would be taken at the top, with views before us to the north and west, panoramas of islands in glittering seas or distant hills ranging away in a milky light. And then, while the men who meant business set off, sometimes for a ten mile stalk or more, Rab and I would slowly descend through the honey-smelling heather, exulting in the scenes that met our eyes. Once, when we took our small white rough-haired Jack Russell terrier with us, we watched amazed as a golden eagle hovered above, perhaps less than a hundred feet up, mistaking our dog for a lamb.

Rab became passionately fond of trawling for mackerel from the

Gannet. He would sit firmly in the stern hour after hour, a blissful smile upon his face, oblivious of everything except the tug on his line. On one occasion we were leaving our loch and heading for the open sea on a day of strong wind, when one of my grandsons held up the tiller which had come adrift in his hands, leaving us unable to steer. Fortunately Julien was again with us and fixed up an oar to steer by, but Rab remained totally unmoved by this potentially hazardous moment since he had just caught a fine mackerel. He became quite miserly about the mackerel we took back to the house, sternly reprimanding me for allowing the freshly caught fish to be smoked for our supper when there were last year's mackerel still in the deep freeze. One of his daughters-in-law, seeing these frozen mackerel, asked for some to take home with her, but the request was indignantly denied.

He had never experienced this sort of carefree holiday before, doing as he pleased, dressing as he pleased, with only the weather as a guide to behaviour, and it bewitched him. I think almost the happiest time of the day would be after returning, sated with wind and sun from one of our trips, when Rab and I would retire to our rooms – he to sit at his desk before the window of his dressing-room, while I repaired the ravages of the day at the dressing-table in our bedroom – both with the same view of the moors to the east, on which the sun would still be shining, chatting together through the open door between us, while the sounds of Mrs Campbell preparing supper below came up through the floor and the prospect of a long evening lay invitingly ahead.

Before going to bed we would stand outside our front door, where the sheep-cropped grass grew up to the house. Rab would probably be wearing his old blue seaman's jersey with a brown tweed jacket, which he put on as a concession for our evening meal. If it was a fine night, a soft wind would be blowing from the north, where the house faced, and the light from Ardnamurchan would gleam as it flashed its warning out to sea. Westward, on our left, the remains of the sunset would light the sky behind the stunted fir trees which sheltered us on that side of the house. To the east the Frachadil burn (always referred to as the Tweed by Rab) would keep up its gentle chatter, the only sound on such a night beyond the whispering of the firs. There would be stars, brilliant in these wide skies, and sometimes the moon would heave itself up behind the line of moors on our east.

Our small but charming bedroom had windows to east and west, and

Rab always decreed that the one to be opened at night was on the side from which the wind did not blow; we went to sleep to the sound of either the firs or the Tweed.

In the evenings we would sometimes listen to the gramophone and I realized how Rab would have come to love music (which he usually referred to as 'that curious whining sound') if he had ever had time in his busy life. He was very fond of Mozart's Bassoon Concerto, which inevitably, with his love for animals, he called the Baboon Concerto. There is a passage where the orchestra comes in after the bassoon solo when our eyes would meet with pleasure. He would be sitting beside the log fire in a vast armchair, a pile of papers on his knees which he sometimes read or on which he wrote; there was generally a dog or two stretched on the hearthrug and I might be engaged in tapestry work, my ears rejoicing in the immortal sounds from the ancient but excellent gramophone. When we were not alone, there would be games, mah-jong, the intricacies of which caused William to make a trunk call to a friend in London to be reminded of the rules. Or we might attempt bridge. Nanny, who always came to Mull with us and helped in many ways, had played whist all her life and the distance between her expert Women's Institute whist and our family bridge was very small indeed. The only real player was William, who with his wife Caroline was to play bridge into the small hours with the Fellows of Trinity when Rab and I had moved into the Master's Lodge there. Nothing could exceed the happiness of those evenings in Mull.

One year was an exception to all this. In 1964 Rab was Foreign Secretary, and the Foreign Office, fastidious in the care of their minister, sent up a relay of young ladies to type and generally bustle the Foreign Secretary. They arrived with neither clothes nor footwear suitable for Mull, but we gave them of our plenty and their reign did not last long since the Cyprus crisis intervened and Rab had to go back to London. But not without a hitch, for a gale blew and all ferries between us and the mainland were cancelled; the polite disbelief from the great Office of State that no boat or airplane was available provided much amusement. Alas, the weather improved and Rab left us. He telephoned every day from London, where there was a stifling heatwave, to hear that we were surrounded by rain and fog and unable even to walk round the hill behind the house without losing our way. It was a big time for the bridge table.

Rab always referred to the mainland as Scotland, giving Mull the status of a separate kingdom. Indeed the forty-five minutes which it took MacBrayne's ferries to cross the Sound of Mull between Oban and the pier at Craignure gave the feeling of being abroad, cut off in some way even from reality, for the West Highland ambience did somehow constitute a different sort of life, slower, easier, more relaxed, apart. There is a theory that the Spaniards who were wrecked on these shores at the time of the Armada have passed down this attitude of mañana through 400 years to their descendants.

This slowing down of life, of time even, was one of the great joys of our holidays. Perhaps all in all we received most pleasure from the waters that surrounded Mull, either from swimming or going out in our boat. Rab would swim in all weathers. On one occasion he was in the sea while the rest of us shivered on Calgary beach when we noticed the shiny head of a seal, swimming quite close to him, and heard Rab's shouts of, 'Go away,' which the seal eventually obeyed.

Another time we had decided to swim at high tide off the old pier in Calgary Bay, which consisted of vast chunks of stone with rough, slippery steps running down to the water. This was usually deserted, being approached by a muddy track and a broken-down gate, but as we started to undress a party of tourists appeared to look at the view. The children and I retreated to a discreet distance and I suggested to Rab that he might do the same. 'No,' he replied, 'I'm going to undress where I can put my clothes on this boodle,' (his word for a bollard) and proceeded to do so regardless of the clustering strangers. Calgary was the scene of a drama when Rab fell overboard from the *Gannet*. His bad arm made him clumsy getting in and out of a boat, and on this occasion he stepped on the gunwale of the dinghy, which tipped up under his weight, precipitating him fully clothed into the water. I had already come ashore with a previous load and watched, helpless, from the pier as Johnny and Stephen grappled in their efforts to get him back into the dinghy. It was impossible to haul him, over six foot tall and heavy in his gumboots, out of the water, and the story ended with him being towed, hanging on to the dinghy painter, back to the steps, where rather pale and shaken he received a rapturous welcome.

The behaviour of the sea round our shores was of constant interest – the heave and surge of a big swell carried in by the tide from a storm far out in the Atlantic, the enormous waves dashing their spray up the rocks when a storm pounded us, and the total stillness of a calm when there was scarcely movement enough to stir a pebble at the water's edge. On some days curtains of rain followed each other across the hills or beat cruelly down on a grey sea.

Other days, when it had rained incessantly, would be followed by a fine evening of great clarity, and on one such we were able, by some refraction of the light caused perhaps by moisture in the air, to see the actual buildings on the air-strip of Coll, eleven miles across the sea, miraged quite plainly. It was always an occasion of much excitement when the visibility enabled us to see the Outer Hebrides, their mysterious humps of hills ranged all along the western horizon, distant and beckoning. I liked to think that they were so named after the Hesperides, which my OED tells me is 'western' in Greek.

Once in Mull we were visited by a member of my family who had recently suffered the tragedy of a loved one lost in a railway accident. At this heartbreaking time I was often reminded of Tennyson's much quoted lines which begin 'Break, break, break on thy cold grey stones, oh sea' as I watched the waters and thought of nature's indifference in the face of human sorrow, and of how when sorrow comes it is as relentless as those waves beating upon the shore.

I remember only one unenjoyable trip in the *Gannet*. We had been peacefully eating our sandwich lunch, rocking at anchor in Ulva Ferry, when it was suggested on impulse that we should circumnavigate the islands of Ulva and Gometra before going home. The day was not propitious, misty and fairly windy, but my Cassandra-like remarks were ignored and we set off. We had no chart on board and, as a small rain set in, it became difficult to see the white water breaking on the rocks to the west of Ulva, which received the full force of the Atlantic Ocean. Six hours in an open boat with no plumbing or shelter, since the hood in the bows had to be kept down to allow the steersman to see, was an ordeal, but we had two of Rab's young male Scottish cousins on board whose eagle eyes enabled us to steer clear of Ulva's pitfalls, and I had a pocket compass which showed us the entrance back to our own loch Tuah before a thick of rain closed in and blotted it out.

There was a beach on Ulva which, in better weather, we frequently visited, Rab enjoying it because the trip across meant that he could fish, and the rest of us happy to go where we never saw another soul – it was only accessible by sea. Of all the beaches on Mull, the Dogs' Swimming

Pool, the Fairy Beach (our names), the favourite was Langamull, the most difficult to reach since the lane approaching it through Forestry Commission trees had many gates to be opened and shut and finally, about half a mile from the sea, it became impassable to all vehicles save our old Land-Rover, which could negotiate every obstacle, ruts, ditches and water. Nearby Mr and Mrs Paul Scofield had a cottage, and on their rare visits we would skirt round them on the sand so as not to invade their privacy, while they would do the same for us.

It was a marvellous beach, open to the north with Skye and Rhum dominating the horizon, and with great cliff-like boulders behind which to shelter from the wind. The young of both our families, brought up with heated swimming-pools, thought Rab and I were mad as we joyfully plunged into water as stimulating as wine and as clean as the Atlantic from which it came. However, I must add that they courageously followed the example of their elders. The sands were covered in what appeared to be coral; I sent some samples to a marine biology establishment on the mainland who reported that these small, white, many-shaped objects were indeed of a coraline substance, and I collected them as precious mementos. I have them now, with shells from the same beach, tiny, delicate, many-coloured and mother-of-pearl, displayed in dishes in my sitting-room, a permanent reminder of that much-loved bit of the seashore.

Year after year we would occupy the same rocks for lunch after our bathe: indeed there was one flat stone which became Rab's personal property as a seat. Afterwards the books would come out and we lay in the sun reading or just lying, while we waited for our bathing suits to dry before another swim.

Anyone who has lain dozing and dreaming on a sandy beach, surrounded by heather and grass, listening to the lisp and hiss of the incoming tide, with its occasional boom as the waves hit the rocks, will understand the magic of those long afternoons at Langamull . . .

7

A LITTLE LEARNING

A glance at the map of Africa will show what a very long way from Mull is Salisbury, then the capital of Southern Rhodesia. It was, therefore, an astonishing coincidence when, in May 1962, Rab and I stepped from the Comet which had brought us from London to be greeted by the Duke of Montrose with the words, 'How are things in Dervaig?' naming the next village to our house in Mull. What made it all the odder on this hot African tarmac was that the Duke gave it its Gaelic name. He was a member of the Rhodesian Governmental Party, which had come to meet Rab on this, his first official visit to the Federation as Minister for Central African Affairs.

The role of a political wife is no different from that of any other wife, unless she be one who has her own career to pursue. The wife of a politician is lucky in that her husband leads a life in which there is room for her to participate and sometimes help, just by being there and enabling her husband to think aloud. Rab liked me to accompany him on his travels and it was my happiness to do so. Thus I found myself standing beside him in the blazing African sun after a bumpy flight which left me too dazed to mind the chanting of unwelcome from the Africans on the airport balcony. I was purely a passenger, an extra to Rab's luggage as it were, and ignorant, except for what he confided in me, of the problems with which he would be grappling. Rab's political views could be summed up by the words 'consensus', 'continuity' and, in a time of crisis, 'coalition', but never 'confrontation' if it could be avoided. In March of this year Macmillan asked him to take on the seemingly impossible task of trying to save the Federation of Northern and Southern Rhodesia and Nyasaland, of which Rab was to write in his autobiography:

It seemed rather simple to suppose that there were any runs to be made. It occurred to many commentators that there was a reputation to be lost.

However, I accepted out of a sense of duty, and also, I think, out of a sense of adventure . . . The problem involved the livelihood and liberty, the expectations and emotions of nine million people.

In other words those of the Federation which had been formed in 1953 and was now causing concern to the British government because of the desire of Nyasaland to secede from this partnership. Again he wrote:

With the nationalist tide coming in, and independence being given or promised to more and more African countries, it began to appear to Africans, in Nyasaland particularly, but also in Northern Rhodesia, that only the Federal Constitution stood between them and the form of freedom accorded to their fellows elsewhere on the continent.

The problems facing him were profound. The Monckton Commission had made clear the rage for independence which was sweeping Africa (started perhaps by Macmillan's own wind of change speech?) but, as on so many occasions when he had been handed a tricky assignment or an obscure position such as Churchill's offer of the Board of Education as it was then known during the war, he turned the result to triumph.

Unknown to Rab, a Minister of the Crown had previously promised secession to Nyasaland, added to which the refusal of Southern Rhodesia to countenance multiracialism was to deal a death-blow to the concept of Federation. Yet by patient, tireless and sympathetic negotiation he was able to achieve a measure of agreement in the final orderly break-up of the three countries, which has never been properly acknowledged in the eyes of some.

The complications of his task are set out in chapter 10 of his book *The Art of the Possible*. The title of this chapter, 'Large Elephant', was that given to Rab by the African chiefs after his visit to Nyasaland, and translated by Sir Glyn Jones, the Governor, as literally meaning 'sagacious beast', a tribute to his handling of their affairs.

After a stay in Salisbury for Rab to hold preliminary talks with Sir Roy Welensky and his Federal Government, we made a brief visit in Sir Roy's private Dakota aeroplane to the home of Stephen and Ginnie Courtauld. I must say a few words about these cousins, related to us both by marriage and very remarkable people, to whom Rab and I were devoted. They had met when both were in their forties, he unmarried and she a divorced Italian countess, when climbing separately on Mont Blanc. They fell instantly in love and were married by the nearest British Consul, who happened to be my uncle Alan Napier, at that time in Bologna. They set up house at 47 Grosvenor Square, where they entertained endlessly, friends from the arts, diplomacy and the young, for to be young was an immediate passport to their friendship.

I remember dining there with August when Igor Stravinsky was staying with them before a concert he was to give which was being broadcast. The great man dined alone upstairs and, when our dinner party went up to the drawing-room, Ginnie, who was not musical, switched on the wireless to listen to the performance. The sounds it gave out sounded very unlike Stravinsky, but in those long-ago days we were all rather in awe of Ginnie and held our peace until the men came up from the dining-room when Stephen instantly tuned in to the right station, announcing rather scornfully that we had been listening to Bournemouth Radio.

Before the war they had bought Eltham Palace, once a royal home and now a ruin, which they transformed into a vast house to which all their friends and relations were constantly bidden. Stephen took special pride in the great hall, where the hammer-beam roof was restored to its original beauty and, if we found the drive through the trams of South London a trial, the welcome and happiness of the stay made it worth while. After the war, when they had experienced to the full the horrors of bombing, they decided to live abroad, since Ginnie's southern blood craved sunshine, and chose Southern Rhodesia. By an extraordinary coincidence they found some land near Umtali named La Rochelle – this being the name of the place in France from where the Huguenot family of Courtauld had originated – and they decided to build a house there and planned a garden, which became their paradise. They imported a gardener from Kew, under whom worked many of the local Nyasas, and it was Stephen's boast that a tree from every country in the world was planted and grew in that marvellous soil.

They threw themselves with enthusiasm into the idea of a multiracial society round about them, buying more land to establish a community where local Africans could be taught farming. They built an art gallery in Salisbury, where they hung some of their own very considerable paintings, including a Mantegna. They gave funds to the university in Salisbury and were always ready to help in any project designed to further African education or well-being. Ginnie was fastidious about food and had taught her Nyasa cook to produce dishes up to her high European standard, consumed in their dining-room hung with landscapes by Turner, which Stephen had brought from England.

They had welcomed our marriage and now welcomed us in person for two happy days and nights in this enchanting home.

From there we flew to Nyasaland. This superbly beautiful country was reached in two tiny aeroplanes, Rab and me in one, and Rab's advisers and detective in the other. We sat as in a car, Rab and the pilot in the front seats and myself and the luggage behind, and I was delighted to find I could open the window beside me and look down on Africa, not so far below. It was the original of the magic carpet. Our stay at Government House with Sir Glyn and Lady Jones was pure fun. The house was crenellated, a sort of Beau Geste fort cum palace, staffed by charming Nyasas. They were barefooted and wore white uniforms with red sashes and seemed happiest if they were doing something for us; they almost tore our clothes from us to wash and iron them. Every morning we had breakfast on our balcony, above which flapped the Union Jack, while before us stretched views of tree-covered mountains. While Rab had talks with Dr Banda, the African chiefs and the Governor (affectionately known locally as 'Malawi' Jones), Nancy Jones would take me to see a leper hospital and to bathe in Lake Nyasa, where I kept very close to the shore since she told me that there were crocodiles in the water. The Joneses took us for a fascinating walk in the mountains, keeping a sharp look-out for red ants; Ginnie and Stephen Courtauld had warned us that, if attacked by them, there was nothing to be done except remove all one's clothes – immediately. But, though we did indeed meet what appeared to be a running river of these ants marching across our path, we were able to avoid their red peril and also to save the Jones's dogs from them.

All too soon we left our dear host and hostess and flew to Northern Rhodesia, where we stayed in another palatial Government House.

As I look back on our printed programme of this visit, what lingers are memories of the kindness of our hosts, Sir Evelyn and Lady Hone, and of meeting Dr Kenneth Kaunda and his wife, he formidable and less friendly than the enchanting Mrs Kaunda, who came to dine at Government House wearing long white gloves on her beautiful black arms and looking impossibly young to have six children.

Back in Salisbury we stayed in the grandest Government House of all (I believe it is now the home of Mr Mugabe) with Lord and Lady Dalhousie. As he was Governor-General, representing the Queen, much pomp was observed; after dinner the women lined up with Meg Dalhousie and, at a signal, all curtsied to him together before leaving the dining-room, but on their own the Dalhousies entertained us with charming informality.

On our departure for home the *Rhodesia Herald* wrote of Rab: 'So far he has not put a foot wrong.' Back at London airport Rab held a press conference, at which, sitting quietly at the side of the room, I marvelled at his replies to the questions which were thrown at him; he was as agile in catching the ball and throwing it back as though he had just risen from his bed, rather than from a long night in an aeroplane.

We paid three visits to Central Africa while Rab was its Minister, and Dr Kaunda and Dr Banda visited him in London in between them, but inevitably, with the depths of racial feeling that existed between Northern and Southern Rhodesia events moved inexorably towards the end of the Federation.

Not all Rab's patient diplomacy, his statesmanship and wisdom, nor what the *Rhodesia Herald* called 'his extraordinary charm and logic' could prevent it. He wrote afterwards: 'If Southern Rhodesia had . . . adopted a liberal constitution which gave a hope to Africans in the government, the whole story of an economic or indeed political union between the Rhodesias would have been different.' As things turned out, it was considered a great achievement on Rab's part that he managed finally to get all three governments to send representatives to meet those from the United Kingdom at the Victoria Falls Conference in June-July 1963. This met for the purpose of the break-up of the Federation. It was entirely due to Rab that the final act came about without violence or strife, and a great triumph that he had achieved the maximum possible agreement out of this tangle of difficulties. The Cabinet sent him a telegram from London, congratulating him on his handling of this most potentially perilous affair.

During the conference we stayed in the Falls Hotel, close to those thunderous waters, along with all the other delegates. Sir Roy and his party would pass us stony-faced if we happened to meet in a passage or the restaurant, but in private he came to our room and invited us to his, where we continued the friendly association we had had with him in the past. The weather was perpetually sunny and I spent much time with Mrs Winston Field, whose husband had succeeded Mr Whitehead as Prime Minister of Southern Rhodesia. I asked Mr Field where he stood politically and was staggered when he replied, 'To the right of Roy Welensky.' Fond as I was of Roy, I did not know that it was possible to be more right-wing than he.

Two pictures from that visit come back to me. The first is of our flight from London. As we are approaching Livingstone airport the pilot announces that we are ahead of our schedule and he is going to take us down to a few hundred feet above the falls. This he does, banking the plane first to one side and then the other as we all gaze at the splendour below in awe and astonishment.

The second picture is on the ground when Rab and I decide to leave our hotel one evening and visit the floodlit falls. As we approach through the undergrowth, by the aid of the floodlighting filtering through the leaves, I observe that Rab's detective, who accompanies us, is carrying a weapon.

'Why have you got your pistol at the ready, Mr Livings?' I ask.

'In case any wild animals should pounce,' he replied.

Africa!

I should now like to take the reader back to an episode which happened five years earlier, before we were married. This domestic chronicle is in no way intended to be a political one; it would not be possible for me to write it as such, but the nature of the path which opened up before me makes it impossible to describe my life without reference to great political events.

Thus, when on 9 January 1957 I saw the words 'Eden resigns' on a newspaper placard at Liverpool Street Station, my heart sank with a purely selfish sensation, since I took it for granted that Rab would become Prime Minister and that our happy relationship would be much disturbed. It never occurred to me to doubt that this would come about.

So when he telephoned me at lunch time the next day, to say that the Queen had sent for Harold Macmillan, I was stunned, partly by his words and partly by the disappointment in his voice. I was as disapointed for him as it was possible to be.

In his book *The Uncrowned Prime Ministers*, D. R. Thorpe writes: 'R. A. Butler, whom many had seen as the most likely and the best qualified successor to Eden, was passed over in favour of the Chancellor of the Exchequer.' It seemed incredible.

Rab took this reverse with stoic courage, and without any rancour or bitterness. Indeed, when Peter Goldman, who had worked closely with him in the Conservative Research Department, said, 'Sorry you didn't make it, sir,' Rab replied, 'Well, I can always appear in the paddock again and have my points judged.' Meanwhile he set about working to serve the Party to which he had given the past twenty-eight years of his life.

The *Manchester Guardian* wrote: 'Asked whether he was disappointed at being passed over for the Premiership, he replied: "Not at all. It's something to have been *nearly* Prime Minister." The brave humour of it!'

This greatly endeared him to the press, but there were many amongst public and press who were both surprised and angered that he had not been chosen, and presumably there were some members of Parliament who felt the same, since Dame Irene Ward MP wrote to *The Times* saying it had been generally assumed that he would succeed Anthony Eden. Human nature does not 'generally assume' a fact which is inimical to it. Arthur Koestler has said that the British, in peacetime at any rate, tend to prefer safe mediocrity to intellectual brilliance, and James Lees-Milne in his biography of Harold Nicolson writes: 'Cliché-ridden nonentities often makes better politicians than men of intellectual brilliance.' This is not to deny the ability and intellect of Harold Macmillan, but highlights the fear and dislike that some back-benchers felt for this quality of intellect. There was no hiding the fact that Rab had it. Laurence Thompson wrote in the *News Chronicle*: 'Much of the immodesty less intelligent men have found in Butler is due to shyness and to intellectual fastidiousness, which make cant, false feeling, intellectual pretentiousness abhorrent to him. With simple people he is at ease, because they are unpretentious and so is he, in the sense that his intellectual power is such that he does not need to pretend. . . . His approach is partly intuitive, as Baldwin's (his modern political hero) was – "sniffing and snuffling at a problem like an elderly spaniel" in Harold Nicolson's happy phrase. But Baldwin was lazy, mentally and physically, which Butler is not.'

In view of the fact that Rab accepted the office of Home Secretary from Macmillan, it is interesting to read this piece about him, also written by Laurence Thompson, before the appointment was made (I make no excuse for quoting so freely from the newspapers since I feel that the journalists who wrote for them often express my views about him better than I could do myself):

He is a man of extreme complexity, one of the two most fascinating contemporary politicians; the other for very different reasons being Aneurin Bevan . . . unwrapping Butler one finds a series of watertight compartments, admission to one of which leads to none of the others, and with no indication which is the central one . . . It may be that it is with Shaftesbury and Wilberforce, rather than Peel and Disraeli, that Butler is destined to be remembered. He is by nature a reformer because in one of the watertight compartments of which he consists is a very kindly humane man.

A leader in *The Times* that January 1957 asks:

The first of the question marks is the load Mr Butler is now to be asked to carry . . . Presumably his general oversight of the home front on behalf of the Cabinet is to continue. But to this with the leadership of the House of Commons there is now added responsibility for the Home Office . . . the demands on Mr Butler's energies will be severe.

The Times's rather pompous leader writer evidently did not know his man, for on top of all this he cheerfully undertook more burdens, consistently standing in as Deputy Leader during Macmillan's absences so that the *Manchester Guardian* was to write: 'Mr Butler has survived Mr Macmillan's absence with distinction and apparently unflagging energy – indeed one of the extraordinary revelations of the interregnum has been the indispensability of Mr Butler.'

He had always been indispensable and it seems extraordinary to the onlookers at the game that this fact was not more widely recognized. The press knew it, they had praised his boldness and courage as Chancellor of the Exchequer, and R. D. Thorpe knew it when he wrote:

Such political foresight is one of the essentials for a Prime Minister and Butler had that ability to a marked degree. He was an immensely rapid and competent administrator, probably one of the most able, and a fast assimilator of information. He was a superb Chairman, could lead a discussion and terminate a meeting economically. These are invaluable qualities for government at the highest level and not to be underestimated. He was a great strategist.

Here was the answer to the leader writer of *The Times*, who feared for the demands on Mr Butler's energies, but one is left sadly wondering at the decision to ignore these qualities.

For all the fact that he must have been deeply hurt by what occurred in January 1957, he seemed to bounce back and go from strength to strength, so that at the time of our marriage, two and a half years later, he was totally in control of three jobs, Home Secretary, Chairman of the Party and Leader of the House of Commons.

Our day would start with breakfast in bed at 3 Smith Square, his house in Westminster within sound of Big Ben's chimes and with a division bell. When Rab was ready for the day's work, I would hang out of the window, looking down to where his car with his police driver, our friend Mr Cosens, and his detective waited below, to wave him goodbye. To my delight he usually managed to be home for lunch and in the afternoon I would often go with him to the House of Commons.

It was amusing to observe from the gallery his mastery of the Commons from the moment when he strolled in, papers under his arm, inscrutable expression on his face, and threw himself down upon the front bench. He never minded my getting in touch by telephone when he was on the bench and he instructed me how to ask for the policeman behind the Speaker's chair. This officer would announce himself with the cryptic words, 'Back of the chair,' and then take my message.

I enjoyed hearing Rab at Question Time, either Prime Minister's questions, if Macmillan was away, or his own Home Office ones, when he was marvellously adept at defusing awkward queries from the Opposition. It was then that he demonstrated why, as a young Secretary of State before the war, he had been nicknamed by Lloyd George the 'Artful Dodger'. He was generous in sharing his amusement with me when he had scored and would look up to the gallery, where I sat, and laugh. I think the position he loved best was that of Leader of the House; he was fond of using sea terms and would speak of himself as quelling a storm or being on the bridge. Someone has said that the job was tailor-made for him; when he first took it on, the *Economist* wrote, 'His urbanity and wit already promise to be great assets as Leader of the House.'

I quote the *Manchester Guardian* again:

The House always looks forward to his appearances at the dispatch box, knowing that he will be entertaining and probably audacious, possibly indiscreet in some ambiguous fashion. He was not indiscreet yesterday, but he was entertaining at times and at others was infinitely nimble in dealing with Mr Gaitskell and Mr Bevan. ('By maintaining Mr Bevan in Opposition we keep him free to make speeches of a high Parliamentary quality which he would be quite unable to make on the Front Bench.')

Of course it wasn't always plain sailing. Everyone knows now from radio the uproar that ensues when the House is roused, rather like a hive which has been struck on the outside causing the bees inside to react in fury. Then, up in the gallery, I would feel my heart swell with indignation as I watched him wait patiently for the noise to cease. But I never again heard such bitter criticism as Hugh Gaitskell poured on his Budget Speech of autumn 1955, of which the *Sunday Times* wrote: 'Mr Gaitskell's personal attack on Mr Butler last Thursday went far beyond the bounds not only of Parliamentary decency but also of the responsibility expected of a former Chancellor of the Exchequer.' This was the occasion when Rab made his famous remark that Bevan, if still wishing for the Labour leadership, had no need 'to stoop to conquer'. Years later Hugh told me what lay behind his hostility; he had just come from the memorial service of a great friend in St Margaret's Westminster, and all the pent up emotion he had felt there burst out in his furious invective.

I did not always agree with Rab's policies. He gave me a ticket to the Speaker's Gallery for the debate on capital punishment in June 1956, when there was a free vote in the House. During the year in which August was High Sheriff of Essex I had attended two murder trials at the assizes and had become an abolitionist in consequence. I was, therefore, delighted when the House gave a majority to Mr Silverman's bill against capital punishment. Rab made one of his serio-comic remarks when it was over: 'All I can say is that I am glad not to be a lonely postmistress in the Highlands tonight.' He changed his views when he became Home Secretary and had the terrible responsibility of life or death for someone found guilty of murder.

I think that for me the single, most moving time of his period as Home Secretary was listening to the speech he made to the Conservative Conference at Brighton in 1961. There had been much demand both from the public and in Parliament for stronger measures to combat crime. 'Whack the thugs', 'Bring back the cat' were headlines after a debate in the House of Commons when 'the conflict between Mr Butler and some of the members behind him could not be disguised. This was Mr Butler at his most typical and at his best. Without putting a word wrong, with no more than a slight underlining here and there for those with an ear for italics, he managed to make his own feelings clear' (*Manchester Guardian*). The women of the party were specially vociferous in their calls for violence to be met with violence, and they had gathered at the conference that afternoon, stern-faced and resolute in thunderous rows facing Rab. Fearful of the outcome of this motion, I had bought a new hat, for confidence, which happened to have a tassle hanging down the back. 'I see you're wearing a cat-o'-nine-tails, Mollie,' joked John Hare as we walked to the conference hall. I need not have feared. Those fierce-faced ladies were turned by the sweet reason of Rab's lucid arguments, which they listened to in gradually awakening respect, until at the end they gave him and his views an ovation. It was a famous victory. It was also the occasion when Iain Macleod came up to me, tears of emotion on his cheeks, and said, 'Tell Rab I have never heard him make a better speech.'

In March 1976 a leader in *The Times* declared:

In politics it is essential that a policy should be formed by men who see the moves a long way ahead. . . . Since the war the grand master of politics in this regard has unquestionably been Lord Butler. The reason that he stayed at the top of politics for thirty years was that he had always thought through the consequence of every policy at least one stage further than other very able men. . . . It is the quality of forward vision that has always given Lord Butler's personality and intellect such a fascination for students of politics.

It was this forward vision which, nearly twenty years before that leader was written, enabled Rab to be such a successful Home Secretary, to avoid the pitfalls and cope with the crises inherent in the job, as well as to inaugurate the reforms for which he became famous.

However, he did fall into a trap of a sort on the occasion of a great dinner in Madrid. We had gone to Spain for the Whitsun recess in 1960, meaning to spend a leisurely holiday by car, sightseeing, and finishing our tour at Algeciras, where Stephen was doing his 'practical' as a hotelier at the Reina Cristina. Our friends Pepe and Casilda Santa Cruz (he was Spanish Ambassador in London) had opened many doors for us, including the magical *parador* at Granada, where one slept in a cell-like room with white walls, thick white linen on the bed and sparkling taps on the bath, lulled by the splash of the Alhambra fountains. But we had not reckoned on a dinner given by the Spanish Foreign Secretary with Rab as guest of honour. This was a full-dress occasion with the women covered in jewels. To my mortification I had only the tidy frock I had packed for dining alone with Rab. (Later, back in England, and wearing a long white lace dress and diamonds, I met our Madrid hostess again, who exclaimed, 'How chic you are!' She surely thought my tidy frock was my usual evening wear.) But my lapse was as nothing compared to the furore in the English press caused by Rab, who followed our host's speech of welcome with one in which he said, in the mildest terms, that he felt the time had come for Spain to take her place amongst the Western powers. 'But, what did he mean?' demanded the reporter from the *Daily Express*, who came in a specially chartered aeroplane to interrupt our idyllic stay at Granada; 'Franco Spain was still under a cloud of remembered dictatorship, was she not?' This blew over as all storms do, but was an example of the extreme delicacy involved in being Home Secretary.

As his wife I sometimes found myself in quite a prominent position and was proud of a good mark I earned from Sir Lionel Fox, chairman of the Prison Commission. He and I were sitting at a small tea-table with the Duke of Edinburgh after the latter had opened a police college in Rab's presence. While we drank our tea, the Duke enlarged on some ideas of his own regarding reforms, to which I listened politely. Afterwards Sir Lionel said: 'You were very discreet.'

The position of Home Secretary carried a wide variety of duties. One where Rab felt very much at sea was for him to inspect the course over which the Grand National was to be run at Aintree. We stayed with Lord and Lady Sefton at Croxteth, where the first thing that struck us on arrival was the tray of drinks, including champagne, on a table immediately inside the front door. There were assembled all the great ones of the racing world to whom, no doubt, Rab and I appeared like babes-in-the-wood. I remember being grateful that Jock and Betsy Whitney, the American Ambassador and his wife, were fellow guests; in my ignorance I thought it was possible that they were not so much imbued with the inner mysteries of the world of the horse as all the rest of the house party. Both Seftons treated me, at any rate, with the kindly indulgence one accords to a half-wit.

On our marriage the Queen most charmingly invited us to a private luncheon with her at Buckingham Palace not long before Prince Andrew was born. A month or two later Rab and I went to Exeter for him to open a new building at the police headquarters. We travelled down by train, Rab absorbed in Home Office papers all the way until, as the train was pulling into the station, he glanced up at me and, perhaps with thoughts of mayoresses in mauve shoes and orchids, said: 'Those clothes won't do.' I might have been dismayed had I not felt confidence in the fact that the smark dark suit and hat I was wearing were those I had worn for the luncheon at Buckingham Palace, and I therefore kept calm. In any case it was too late to be anything else. During the opening ceremony Rab's detective approached and whispered in his ear the news of the birth of Prince Andrew, according to ancient custom the Home Secretary being the first to be informed. Rab interrupted his speech to announce the good news.

The first state banquet at Buckingham Palace which I attended with Rab took place in April 1960 on the occasion of the visit of President and Madame de Gaulle. This was an event of great delight in marked contrast to my presentation at Court many years before, when, terrified by the solemnity of the occasion and wearing feathers and a train, I curtsied to an unsmiling Queen Mary. She was alone since King George was not well, but I was at the time certain, no doubt mistakenly, that this was not the cause of her apparent displeasure, but something wrong in my demeanour.

Now, in the reign of her granddaughter, the Court presented a very different face, happy, relaxed, made easy by the charming manners of the courtiers and dazzlingly beautiful to the eye. My enjoyment of the succession of courses, served on gold plates and exquisite Sèvres, was slightly diminished by the fact that on one side of me was seated Sir Winston Churchill. I naturally wished to keep up an intelligent flow of talk with this great man (Rab had told me I should do well if I did not have to descend to discussing his goldfish), but. alas, his speech was impaired that evening and conversation was difficult. Worse was to come. When, after the Queen's speech of welcome, the President rose to reply in his sonorous French tongue, Sir Winston turned to me and, while de Gaulle was actually speaking, said imperiously, 'Twanschlate!'

I murmured 'Later,' and was thankful that he then forgot me and all thoughts of translation.

Rab was not fond of the theatre, the cinema or the concert hall, though he would go, under duress, to Covent Garden when the kind Droghedas invited us to the Royal Box. (Sadly the only form of entertainment he really enjoyed was one which I cordially disliked, namely the circus, where we were always invited to a box at Olympia by the Bertram Mills family.) One visit to the theatre which he could not avoid was when we were to accompany the Queen, as guests of M. Chauvel. The French Ambassador had many guests that night, but honoured us with seats beside Her Majesty. The play, in French, was by Anouilh. The story revolved round twins, a cheerful one who always held his head up, and a melancholy one, his head hanging down on his chest. They were both played by the same actor, who received enormous applause when he took his curtain call, but Rab demanded, 'Where is the other one?'

At the party afterwards the Queen, who had sat next to Rab in the theatre, said somewhat acidly to me, 'I thought Mr Butler understood French?'

'Yes, Ma'am, he was partly educated in France.'

'Well, he didn't seem to understand what was going on tonight!'

We often dined out and one occasion stays in my memory. It was at an embassy, a very large party where Rab murmured during the pre-dinner drinks, 'I see many hired waiters here tonight.' At dinner I sat on the Ambassador's left, while Rab was on the hostess's left and, both being engaged at the beginning of the meal with the guest on their right hand, we were free to witness the wonderful scene that followed. A waiter marched in bearing aloft an enormous dish. He tripped and fell, bringing down with him a mass of fish and sauce. A second waiter, hard on his heels and also fish-laden, slipped on the sauce and fell beside the first waiter. It was hilarious. The poor men, grovelling and sliding, had to be helped to their feet and an aproned lady came in to clean up the mess. Rab, when recounting this story, couldn't resist saying that the fish was scraped from the floor before being handed round and that some of the guests were chary of eating it.

If we were not dining out, he would be engaged on his boxes and, half-spectacles on his nose, would talk to me as he ran his eyes down his papers before initialling them in red ink.

Years of such reading meant that he was very apt to run his eyes down, rather than along, the pages of his less serious reading (I would occasionally catch him out over details which he had missed if we were both reading the same book). But, alas, we did not often agree about the books we enjoyed. For example there was Mr Woodhouse and Mr Wodehouse, one the father of Emma and the other father of a whole world of creatures from another existence. Virginia Woolf writes in her *Common Reader*:

The wit of Jane Austen has for partner the perfection of her taste. Her fool is a fool, her snob is a snob, because he departs from the model of sanity and sense which she has in mind, and conveys to us unmistakably even when she makes us laugh. Never did any novelist make more use of an impeccable sense of human values. It is against the disc of an unerring heart, an unfailing good taste, an almost stern morality, that she shows up those deviations from kindness, truth and sincerity which are amongst the most delightful things in English literature.

This piece of mandarin writing expresses views with which all of those who love and admire Jane Austen can agree, and there is another aspect, the one which Leslie Hartley illuminated in his talk to the Royal Society of Literature, 'Jane Austen and the Abyss'. He enlarged on a side which is often forgotten, a side which Charlotte Brontë in her well-known criticism denied, the part of Jane Austen which faces and describes the terror of life, the terror of rejection and loneliness. This was something which Marianne Dashwood knew in her broken love-affair with Willoughby, which little Fanny Price experienced in her childhood, and which Jane Austen must have experienced herself, for her words are authentic.

I have read her at all times in my life and always with the same reward, but this was something I couldn't share with Rab; he couldn't catch her flavour. The same embargo existed on the very different esoteric world of P. G. Wodehouse. Rab didn't wish to enter either of them, although I once brought tears to his eyes by reading aloud to him 'Lord Emsworth and the Girl Friend'. His sister Dor and I, equally at home with both these writers, would cap each other's quotations about Gussy Fink-Nottle, Aunt Dahlia and Bertie, Mrs Bennett and Miss Bates in happy agreement. It is sometimes a comfort in life to have the escape route which these characters provide.

As we grew older, Rab and I both found that we wept more easily, and there was one subject which Rab could not mention without tears; this was the Battle of Jutland when Lord Jellicoe, in an old macintosh, had given some order to the Fleet which Rab found particularly moving. (Once, at Spencers, I was called by Susie with the words, 'Come quickly. Rab is crying!' I found him in the library with a *Life of Jellicoe*, which had belonged to August.) Another cause for tears was the identification of something loved with a poem. In December 1975 the Queen came to a poetry reading given to commemorate the 150th Anniversary of the Royal Society of Literature, of which Rab was President, held in Skinners Hall. Among the readers were Sir John

Betjeman and Jill Balcon, who chose as one of her readings Kipling's 'The Way through the Woods'. I knew this lovely and evocative poem well and felt sure that Rab, on hearing it, would think of his loved Gatcombe woods and be moved to tears. He was seated next to the Queen with myself further along the row, and glancing secretly at him I saw that, as I expected, he was mopping his eyes with a handkerchief while the Queen eyed him enquiringly.

His love of books was idiosyncratic. He had not had much time in his busy life for novels (he refused to read those of George Eliot because he thought her such an ugly woman), but one exception was Tolstoy's *War and Peace*, which he admired. Prominence has been given to this fact by one of his former Principal Private Secretaries, now an ambassador, who claimed in a book and in a television appearance that Rab's favourite character in literature was Pierre Bezukov. ('His attitude in dealing with the French invasion was to delay and withdraw. I think I am rather like him,' Rab is quoted as saying.) The author is mistaken. Rab's favourite character from this gigantic book was Marshal Kutuzov, the wonderful old man who was made Commander-in-Chief of the Russian armies, 'who cannot sit a horse, who drops asleep at a Council' and who was the victor of Napoleon at the battle of Borodino. *He* indeed may have been a little like Rab. Another favourite was Meredith and I staggered through *The Egoist* merely to please him. There is a list of suggested reading which he wrote in an elegant hand at the age of twenty-four (emulating the Emma Woodhouse he despised). It includes Froude's *Caesar*, Paul Bourget's *Essais de psychologie contemporaine*, Hardy's *Dynasts*, Doughty's *Arabia, Creed of a Tory* by Loftus, *Asiatic Studies* by Lyall and *Travel Diary of a Philosopher* by Keyserling. No wonder Stanley Baldwin had warned him, while still at Cambridge, of the sin of intellectualism, at the same time handing him 'a shocker', as Rab called it, from the station bookstall. He read history with pleasure and often returned to Gibbon's *Decline & Fall*, Vasari's *Lives*, and F. S. Oliver's *The Endless Adventure*. His two favourite poems were the 'Elegy in a Country Churchyard' and Keats's 'La belle dame sans merci' – he loved Keats so much that he placed him above Shakespeare. He had absorbed much French literature during his education in France between school and Cambridge, and was familiar with Stendhal, Balzac, Flaubert and Montaigne, so familiar with the latter that he had discovered indecent bits which he would quote to me.

But not even to please me would he read my favourite Proust. After I had read *A la recherche du temps perdu* three times in Scott-Moncrieff's translation I tried him in French, but I was constantly checked by unknown words. I would then turn to Rab, who astonished me by replying, 'It's not French.' In fact I was told by an excessively well-educated Frenchwoman that Proust did not write like a Frenchman, so no doubt Rab was right. He used to lament that Greek literature had been omitted from his education, saying bitterly, 'I never even read the "Death of Socrates".'

He was proud of his position as President of the Royal Society of Literature, and would take the chair in the Society's fine house north of the Park whenever a talk was being given by one of its members, distinguished authors and people prominent in the arts. He gave a lecture there himself on 'The Prevalence of Indirect Biography', but since it was not a political speech I could not get him to take much trouble with the script, which he delivered in a monotonous voice without raising his eyes from his paper. He invited me to give a talk which, with some trepidation, I did, speaking of 'A Personal Proust.' I was honoured by George Painter, the celebrated biographer of Marcel Proust, coming to take the chair for me, and by the President sitting in the front row. Afterwards Carola Oman wrote a note saying she had enjoyed my lecture on 'that deplorable Frog' and Freddy Birkenhead, a Proustian, congratulated me in a letter which I treasured.

If on a hot afternoon Rab's eyes would be shut during such proceedings and his mind appear to wander, he would confound everyone at the close by his succinct summing up and drawing together of all the ends in his own masterly fashion.

8

A Dangerous Thing

There were those who admired Mr Macmillan, and others who were less enthusiastic about him. I have always belonged to the latter category. From the first I found his assumption of old-world courtesy insincere and the coldness of his eyes belied, to me, any show he might make of possessing a heart. The only man whose eyes were equally cold, though with a quite different expression, was President Kennedy, whom I met briefly on his state visit to London. I did not think that Mr Macmillan, if he ever went for a country walk, would return with wild flowers in his pocket, as Rab did for me.

It has been suggested that Rab was privy to the 'night of the long knives' in July 1962 when the Prime Minister got rid of a third of his Cabinet, in Rab's words, 'the most drastic reorganization of a government ever undertaken within the lifetime of a modern parliament'. Beyond a hypothetical discussion with the PM at lunch a week before this took place on the merits of bringing in younger men, Rab, was, I will not say unaware that changes were about to take place, but certainly ignorant of the size of the sackings and dismayed by their result, of which he wrote, 'The spilling of so much blood did serious damage to the Prime Minister's hitherto unbroken image of "unflappability".' He was saddened to lose so many old colleagues, but writes, 'I was personally unwounded . . . by the massacre of Glencoe,' although Macmillan required from him the post of Home Secretary, which he gave to Henry Brooke. We realized that the so-called honours which were now laid upon Rab – Deputy Prime Minister, First Secretary of State – were but empty titles. What I, at any rate, did not fully realize at the time was the fact that they were designed to tie him more closely to the Prime Minister, allowing the latter to make every use of Rab's well-known loyalty, both to him personally and to the Conservative Party. In June 1963 I sat next to Macmillan at a state banquet for the President of India at Buckingham Palace. It was soon after the tragedy of the Profumo affair, which led to what Rab called 'a crisis of confidence in the House of Commons', adding, 'When I talked to the PM he was not in a happy mood and resigned to the fact that he would probably have to go.' We know that Macmillan did not go, but on this occasion he aired his views to me about resigning, no doubt, leading me up the garden path. I, perhaps thinking aloud, said that I supposed in those circumstances he would go to the House of Lords, to which his lofty reply was, 'I do not receive honours, I give them.'

When I learnt, just before the Conservative Party Conference in October 1963, that the Prime Minister had been taken ill, I could not prevent the thought that entered my mind: had Rab's turn come at last? The same thought had evidently crossed the minds of the press, who were there in hordes to take our picture as we boarded the train for Blackpool.

It was an unhappy conference. Macmillan's absence obviously caused upheaval and Rab, who had stood in so often for him before, was manifestly the person to take control during its deliberations and beyond . . . but there were many rivals, and the atmosphere of intrigue which permeated the rooms and corridors of the hotel where we stayed was disagreeable. The heightened atmosphere, the tension, the lack almost of decorum was something which I had not experienced before, but I suppose that it was inevitable after the announcement of Macmillan's resignation had been publicly read to the conference from the platform. Rab said in an interview later that he felt this announcement caused the most unsatisfactory and disturbing situation, adding that he was criticized at the time for trying to maintain the position of Macmillan, but that he was overtaken by events. He thought that the issue of whether Macmillan could or could not go on as Prime Minister was not one to be raised at the Party Conference, adding, 'I am not thinking about myself, or whether I got it or not [the leadership], but that you should not insert into a Party Conference the question of the designation or election of a new leader.'

I spent much of my time sitting on the landing outside our hotel bedroom while the Tory 'top brass' were inside, discussing with Rab the speech he was to make on the closing afternoon in Macmillan's place; he had had to insist that it would be he who would make it and no one else. Alec Home very kindly suggested at one stage that I might like to use his sitting-room while ours was so occupied, and Tom Bridges (one of his private secretaries who later became Rab's, and is now Ambassador in Rome) hastily locked the Foreign Office boxes as I entered the room. Looking back on those days of perfect autumn weather beside a gentle and smiling sea when I went often to the many cocktail parties by myself, I now realize that a great deal of the jostling and manoeuvring was going on behind our backs. Rab was too busy to regard much of it, and I suppose I was pitifully ignorant of the pain of politics and simply looked forward to the time when my husband would step into the shoes which had so long awaited him.

Alec and Elizabeth Home were friends, not rivals in our eyes, and thus we were both amazed when, lunching with us before Rab's speech, Alec told us he was going to see his doctor because he had been asked to stand as leader.

I never knew how much this revelation affected the speech Rab made that afternoon to the packed hall of the conference. The words he used had all been decided before he made it – but the manner? I had heard him on so many occasions and I knew that this was not the best that he could do. It was as though he was too fastidious to make the sort of speech which would arouse enthusiasm, set the delegates on fire, such as I had often heard him make on smaller occasions, and though I was told by others how well the speech *read*, I knew in my heart that it was not what the rank and file in the hall wanted or those on the platform hoped for. Something seemed to be holding him back from giving his real self (the invisible presence of the sick man in London?) and his heart was not in it as it would have been had he stood there as leader in reality. Long afterwards, speaking to Kenneth Harris on television, Rab said, 'I was tempted in the speech I made . . . on Saturday at Blackpool to express my feelings. But I thought the honest course in public life in Britain was to make your speech, and let people infer or deduct or abstract or think what they like. And I did that with absolute honesty and therefore I made my speech without making any personal revelations at all. And if you think that's wrong, then I think you underestimate the honesty and the straightforwardness with which some of us conduct our political life.'

The *Guardian* was kind enough to be sympathetic: 'How Mrs Butler must have hated the conference,' they wrote.

We travelled back to London in the same railway compartment as

Lord Dilhorne, the Lord Chancellor, who maintained, whether he really believed it or not, that Rab's chances of succeeding Macmillan were excellent.

The next day, Sunday 13 October, there appeared an article by William Rees-Mogg entitled 'The week of wounding' (*Sunday Times*), in which he wrote: 'Here at Blackpool, Mr Butler, the acting Prime Minister, seems almost alone to have had any time to attend to Her Majesty's business, and he has been put in a most invidious position to conduct it', and he ended his article with the words:

But the memory of a week in which Mr Butler's conduct alone seemed that of a wholly adequate leader (certainly he was the only man who looked at all like a Prime Minister) is going to stick for a long time in the minds of those who went through it. Only at the very end, at the mass meeting, did the ordinary delegates make their own bid for unity. They were not all Mr Butler's supporters, but they all applauded his very fine speech to show that they were prepared to unite behind a suitable leader.

We returned to London to a suite in St Ermin's Hotel since there was dry rot in our house in Smith Square (as well as in the body politic). This place will be forever connected in my mind with the coming failure of Rab's hopes and the nightmare of watching that failure come about, though the word failure could never be applied to Rab himself, whose conduct throughout demonstrated his great courage and dignity. The days from 14 October until it was all over on Saturday the 19th were those of fierce trial. All the while Rab was working at 10 Downing Street, attending to the business of Government for the absent Prime Minister, while the press kept up a see-saw of headlines: 'The people's choice', 'Butler tops the poll', 'It's deadlock' were some of them, and with our hopes came the suspicion that these hopes were not well founded.

By Thursday 17 October a name had 'emerged' as being the most likely successor to Macmillan, and it was not Rab's, but that of Alec, Lord Home. During that day support for Rab solidified amongst his Cabinet colleagues and there were feverish telephone calls and meetings until evening, when the famous gathering in Enoch Powell's house took place. Here all the previous contenders and rivals met together, sinking their own differences in their determination that Rab, and no one else, should be their leader. One and all they telephoned this message to St Ermin's Hotel, where I was alone (I have been unable to remember, and

patient research by others has failed to discover, where Rab had gone).
Wearily I wrote on the hotel blotting paper, since there did not seem to
be any writing paper, the names of Iain Macleod, who was leader of the
House of Commons, Lord Aldington, Joint Chairman of the Party,
Reggie Maudling, Chancellor of the Exchequer, and Freddy Erroll,
President of the Board of Trade, who all wanted Rab and wanted to tell
him so. Another voice on the telephone, though not from Enoch's
house, was that of Quintin Hogg (he had just renounced his peerage as
Lord Hailsham), who roundly remarked of the name of Alec Home,
'Mollie, this simply will not do!' Sometime during that evening I was
told that Edward Boyle was flying to London to demonstrate his support
for Rab, while early next morning, as Rab was shaving and I was still in
bed, came a telephone call from Lord Lambton in the north to protest
against anyone other than Rab becoming Prime Minister. But on this
fateful Friday things were to move fast. Martin Redmayne, the Chief
Whip, who had attended the previous night's 'cabal', reported what had
happened there to Macmillan, which accelerated events. The sick man
promptly requested the Queen to visit him in hospital. Her Majesty
called there at 11.15 a.m., accepted his resignation and thereafter sent
for Lord Home to the palace.

I lunched with Rab at the Carlton Club, where we sat at the table
immediately to the left of the dining-room door. Across the room were
seated, amongst others, two firm supporters of Rab's – William Rees-
Mogg and Humphry Berkeley. How great must have been their
excitement, at this moment of crisis, to see the one crucial figure
lunching opposite them. As they passed us on their way out, they
stopped and William said, 'I do hope, sir, that you are going to refuse to
serve.' Humphry then went to the coffee-room, where he found Peter
Goldman; in an effort to persuade him, they both returned to our table,
where, in Peter's words, 'Rab was looking Delphic'. But William's
words were all that I remembered as we drove to 10 Downing Street,
where Rab went directly after lunch for discussions with Lord Home.
As Rab got out of the car the crowd on the pavement gave him a great
ovation. That roar of welcome was my undoing: I was melted by the
people's love for him. My tears were those of intense emotion, caused
partly, as I have said, in reaction to the crowd and partly by my grief for
Rab, who, I felt sure, would eventually agree to serve and thus give up
the crown with which I longed for him to be rewarded.

That afternoon the *Evening Standard* reported:

The choice of Lord Home is regarded as a deliberate attempt to stop Mr R. A. Butler from becoming Prime Minister. The rebels believe . . . and in this they are supported by the latest *Daily Express* and Gallup polls of public opinion, that Mr Butler commands a wide measure of support in the country and could well pull off an election victory.

And in another column:

There has been a disturbing atmosphere of *après moi le déluge* about the astonishing last hours of Mr Macmillan's reign. He can be admired for his courage in days of sickness and crisis, but he cannot be praised for the way he has railroaded party opinion with his own preferences and prejudices.

These views were all widely expressed by the press and I knew them, in my heart, to be true.

That night we were visited in our hotel by Rab's oldest friend and colleague, Geoffrey Lloyd, who had been with him at Cambridge and in Government. Another visitor was John Junor, editor of the *Sunday Express*, and they and I together tried into the small hours to persuade Rab that there was still a chance. Everyone knew that Lord Home could not form a government without him, would he not hold out? But our words were in vain. Rab had never sought anything for himself and he could not act out of character at this most crucial time of his career. I felt that he was putting loyalty to his party above loyalty to his country, but I was wrong. I think that to him the two were synonymous. On that Saturday morning *The Times* leader ran: 'It seems prodigal of the Conservative Party at this juncture in its affairs to pass over the experience, toughness, record of departmental success, and sheer political acumen that Mr Butler has to offer.' While the *Daily Mail*'s comment was: 'Mr Butler is thought to be too "progressive", yet it is these enlightened policies . . . which won the Conservatives their third successive victory in 1959.'

But it was all too late. At 10.30 that morning Rab went to 10 Downing Street and in the Cabinet room, where he had so often presided, agreed to serve in Alec Home's government. Neither of us had lost our feelings of friendship for the Homes, and later Alec and Rab wrote each other civilized and comradely letters, which Rab's biographer quotes in full. But it would be naïve to pretend that I was unaware of whose manoeuvres had prevented Rab from becoming Prime Minister; I vowed privately never to speak to Harold Macmillan again. As the train took us away to Gloucestershire that evening I looked out at the fields and hedges on which the darkness was coming down, and reflected sadly to myself (Rab was temporarily locked away from me in the harsh aftermath of his decision) that history had taken a wrong turning and that England had lost a great Prime Minister that day. In years to come there would be many who would echo this thought. But the bitter disappointment which I felt for so great a man and so dear a husband could not obscure the knowledge that his place in history was secure and had even been enhanced by his conduct.

Meanwhile we were both overwhelmed with letters, by far the majority of which were from strangers, all expressing their praise for Rab's handling of the struggle and disappointment at its outcome. Christopher sent three extremely outspoken telegrams from Cambridge during the week of uncertainty.

I have described this amazing episode as it appeared to me, but this was by no means the last word. Iain Macleod, who with Enoch Powell refused to serve in the new government, wrote an article for the *Spectator* which became famous. It was entitled 'The Tory Leadership' and Rab said of it that every word was true. I need only quote one sentence from it: 'The truth is that at all times, from the first day of his Premiership to the last, Macmillan was determined that Butler, although incomparably the best qualified of the contenders, should not succeed him.' Years later Rab, talking to Kenneth Harris, explained how his decision had been taken:

You can't alter your own nature, and I think that's a very important rule for people in life – to live according to their own nature. And while I was very much pressed at the time, I felt that if I had been invited by a majority, I would have been glad to serve, but it wasn't according to my nature to force myself if I was not chosen by a majority, and that must be according to your own likes, and I would have thought that I couldn't really have expressed it any more in public than I did. I decided not to make personal revelations or personal statements in my speech to the Party because I thought it was not according to the tradition of British politics: to push one's own self when one was there to make a lead for the Conservative policy and philosophy . . . It may be wrong, and I may have paid for it, but I have at least stuck to my own principles and my own ideals, and I think this is very important in life.

I find this lonely voice of altruism, speaking across the years, very moving.

Humphry Berkeley, in telling us of the loaded manner in which the Chief Whip had been instructed to question members of Parliament as to their preference, was responsible for a 'Rabism'. When Martin Redmayne was made a director of the House of Fraser, Rab murmured, 'I never dare go into Harrods these days in case I meet him walking about in a tail-coat!' His light-hearted words shall be the last about these old unhappy far-off things as I turn to the sunshine of nearly a year when Rab was Foreign Secretary, the place which Alec Home immediately offered him.

Enoch Powell has written of Rab that he 'needed position and authority to put forth his full capabilities – provided the mantle was placed around his shoulder, he would wear it to the manner born. I can remember how once, during the long period when he was Chairman of the Home Affairs Committee of the Cabinet, he was absent ill for a week or two, and someone else occupied the chair. It was as if Government itself came to a standstill. Unrivalled in dispatch of business, he was firm, subtle, and determined as leader of a team. Rab was cast in the proconsular mould, born to occupy office, swimming in it like a huge fish and gasping, stranded when it eluded him.' Wonderfully apt words. It had been Rab's ambition for years to be Foreign Secretary but, alas, with an election coming within a year, there was not long for him to enjoy it. He himself quoted, in a lecture in Australia, Talleyrand's description of an ideal Foreign Secretary:

A Minister for foreign affairs must be endowed with a sort of instinct which gives him such quick warning that it prevents him from compromising himself in any discussion. He must have the faculty to appear open while remaining impenetrable, he must be reserved yet capable of letting himself go, he must be subtle in choosing his methods of amusing himself. His conversation must be simple, varied, unexpected, always natural and sometimes naif.

I can recognize Rab in much of these words. He has set down in his book his aims:

My desire to ease the warlike or semi-warlike situation in Cyprus and Borneo and Aden was achieved with the aid of the Commonwealth Secretary, Duncan Sandys . . . I wanted to test the reality of our special relationship with the USA and lastly to find out from the Soviet leaders what chance there is or was of

Mollie Montgomerie in 1930

August Courtauld in 1930

August in Greenland 1935

On the same trip, Mollie Courtauld watches an Eskimo woman skin a polar bear

August, on leave in 1940, at a meet of the hounds with six-year-old Christopher, who was able to keep up for an eight-mile point that day

August studying a chart on board his ship, 1942

The family at Spencers, 1944: (*back row, left to right*) Dorothy Napier, Christopher (9), Mollie with William (1), Alan Napier; (*front row*) Stephen (4), Esmé Montgomerie, Perina (11), Frank Douglas Montgomerie and Julien (6)

The children in 1951: (*back row*) William (*left*) and Christopher; (*front row*) Julien, Perina holding Susie, and Stephen

Pamela Havsteen-Mikkelsen with her son Alan in occupied Denmark, 1940

Spencers

On their wedding day in October 1959: Mollie and Rab Butler

On honeymoon in Rome, Rab points out the Keats and Shelley memorial house from the Spanish steps

Rab in Saffron Walden cattle market with his agent Kenneth Baker and a farmer friend, 1959

Launching the tanker *Gulf Briton* in 1960 with Charles Clore

At a village fête in the constituency

On Mull, trying to avoid the press, 1960

Frachadil undergoing repairs. (*Left to right*) Susie, Sarah, Mollie and Rab

Rab, in typical pose, working at 10 Downing Street during Macmillan's illness in 1963

At the Conservative Party Conference, Blackpool, 1963

During the leadership crisis in October 1963

Rab in Nevile's Court, Trinity College, Cambridge

At sea off Mull, 1977

Christopher at the helm of *Duet* passing the Fastnet Rock during a race for 'old gaffers', 1975. *Duet* was first round the rock, but was beaten on handicap

Mollie Butler with (*above, left to right*) Perina, Christopher and Julien; and (*below, left to right*) Stephen, William and Susie

POSTCARDS to Cummings

(1) As deputy Prime-Minister, though it time to try on Prime-Minister's clothes — tweeds tickle and Macmillan tartan draughty underneath / yours RAB/Mull

relaxation of tension in the nuclear age. These then were my objectives.

Everyone who has written about Rab has commented with pleasure and affection on his indiscretion. (I remember when I first got to know him well being astonished at what he would say on the telephone from his Ministry, regardless of the switchboard.) He used to meet the Lobby correspondents of the House of Commons upstairs on a Thursday afternoon from about 1946 to 1962, and has said that they enjoyed the half hour he spent with them as much as he did. He wrote:

Here I found innumerable friends such as David Wood of *The Times* and Boyd of the *Guardian*. Though cheerful and on the verge of discretion, never once did any of that band let me down or mention me by name. Very often on the Friday morning there were columns conveying my impressions of the Government's or the Opposition's attitude and very few knew the source.

Nicko Henderson, who succeeded Oliver Wright as Rab's Principal Private Secretary at the Foreign Office, has written:

The press naturally loved Rab's unfailing indiscretions as did the Office. Young Counsellors from the departments, summoned to his room for a discussion on some burning issue, for example Cyprus, were astonished to hear him giving his views on his Cabinet colleagues, on the Conservative Party or the conduct of Cabinet business.

It was a most lovable trait. But on anything secret he remained secret.

Nicko Henderson was an extremely attractive youngish man, sophisticated, quiet, highly intelligent, attentive to Rab and charming to me. We saw a lot of him, as he accompanied Rab on all our tours abroad and he and his wife Mary generally came to help with our official luncheons. She, later a popular ambassadress, is a considerable artist and for many years we received Christmas cards from their various posts drawn by her.

We soon moved into the Foreign Secretary's official home in 1 Carlton Gardens, which consists of a dining-room on the ground floor, where we gave many luncheons and dinners, a rather pompously furnished drawing-room above it for official entertaining and, above this, reached by a lift, our private rooms. These last were a soulless abode, furnished and decorated by the Ministry of Works with their usual lack of taste and imagination, and leaning towards the colour of porridge for walls and materials. Our own possessions were still in store after the renovation of 3 Smith Square, so my mother gave us some of her china to cheer up the general effect. Even so, the young Frenchwoman who came on some mornings for conversation to brush up my French, gazing around our sitting-room, murmured, '*Cette pièce est un peu vide.*'

Here I was to have my first taste of Government hospitality, which provided the sort of help I had never imagined existed. It was presided over by a delightful Brigadier, Geoffrey Macnab, for whom nothing was too much trouble. ('You liked the champagne in the box at the Derby? We'll find out what it was and have it for the dinner this week.') The head butler was a Mr Pettifer ('Petit Fours' to the Brigadier), who had been with Queen Mary at Marlborough House when she was a very old lady. He confided to me that he had found the tedium of meals there almost intolerable; the Queen would generally be alone with one lady-in-waiting, who would read to her during the meal, while Mr Pettifer stood behind her chair. Tall and imposing, he was a most wonderful character who exuded confidence, enabling one to relax, however important or foreign the guests, in the knowledge that his infinitely experienced hands were guiding the occasion. Meanwhile, Geoffrey Macnab would have provided the perfect meal and wines, and I generally asked him to ensure that the flowers were the colours of our guest's national flag.

At Carlton Gardens or at Lancaster House many were the jokes Rab and I exchanged with Geoffrey as we waited for our guests, who, during this whirlwind year, seemed to come from every country in the world.

Looking back on the programmes of those meals, with a red hand stamped on them pointing to one's position at the table, I cannot believe that there was a single ambassador I did not sit beside. We both loved entertaining and, of course, in such easy circumstances there was nothing to fear except the exhaustion of constant duties, visits abroad, official dinners, speaking engagements, tea-parties for ambassadors' wives and theatre parties for visiting foreign dignitaries. Not a day was totally free and my head reels as I look back over the lists which Rab's secretary prepared for us each week. Our very first engagement was to take the President of Iceland to the Old Vic to see *Hamlet* in its entirety. This was quite a test, but was lightened by Nicko, who appeared wearing black velvet slippers embroidered 'I. F.' He was a friend of Ian Fleming's.

The trips abroad which were to make this year so enjoyable started with a visit to The Hague in October and another to Denmark the following January. This latter was particularly happy for me since my sister had married a famous Danish painter, Sven Havsteen-Mikkelsen, and they were at all the parties given for us, while the daughter of our old friends, Ebbe and Kirsten Munck, was married to the young diplomat from the Danish Foreign Office who was in attendance on Rab. All Danes speak good English and there is a press photograph of an audience roaring with laughter at some joke Rab has made during a speech. On a particularly icy January day we were driven out to Elsinore and were suitably chilled going round the ramparts of Hamlet's castle.

Next month we paid our first visit, as Foreign Secretary and his wife, with Alec and Elizabeth Home to Canada and the USA. Nicko Henderson has written that we inevitably felt 'out of it' travelling with the Prime Minister and his staff, but I do not remember this feeling; only a sense of excitement in the special aeroplane, a Comet, with its load of secretaries and shorthand-typists. The plane landed in Iceland, where there was a lengthy wait in an uncomfortable shed-like building, while it was de-iced. At Ottawa, at any rate, I felt far from out of it: immediately I had followed my betters down the steps of the aeroplane, I was clasped in a bear-like hug by Mrs Nell Martin, wife of the Canadian Foreign Secretary, whom I had never met before.

We stayed at Government House with Georges Vanier, whose wife was absent, visiting a village in France which was founded by her son for mentally handicapped children. All I saw of this sunlit and snow-covered city was the Canadian National Gallery, before we flew on to Washington. Here, at a dinner at the White House, I sat next to President Johnson and, as Nicko has described slightly inaccurately in his book, was inundated with signatures from the President on every scrap of paper he could lay his hands on, place cards, menus, etc. Keen politician that he was, he told me he was pleased with the way Rab's talks with the Secretary of State, Dean Rusk, had gone. Afterwards there was dancing and I was a little disconcerted, as I circled the room with Rab, when the President stepped in, piloted me once round the room before whirling me from him, explaining that he could thus dance with every woman present.

Elizabeth Home took me with her to pay a call on the recently-widowed Jackie Kennedy in a delicious old red brick house; she was unexpectedly coy in her mannerisms while giving us morning coffee. But I received a terrifying example of the Kennedy clan's cold-blooded confidence during a tea-party at the British Embassy when the indomitable Rose, mother of the murdered Jack, said with brutal firmness that her son Robert would be the next President.

Rab and I flew to New York in a snowstorm in the last plane to leave before the aerodrome was shut by the snow, and somehow we were separated from our luggage. Arriving in the hothouse atmosphere of our suite (the President's) at the top of the Carlyle Hotel, I had only the fur-lined boots in which I had left Washington, and the heat was such that I went down in the lift for our lunch with Adlai Stevenson, the United States Ambassador to the UN, in stockinged feet. But the memory of this mortification is not so strong as that of the wonderful sunset, seen from our palatial suite high above the city that afternoon. We flew back on 14 February, when a home-made Valentine was brought to me from further back in the plane; I was delighted to discover it was from Nicko.

Our next visit to stay with the Harlechs at the Washington Embassy was on the way to Japan and the Philippines. We broke the journey at Honolulu, where the private secretaries and others of the staff were able to bathe from the famous beach while Rab and I, yearning to do the same, had to squash into a small English car and be driven to visit some of the English residents in their suburban villas. It was frustrating to say the least. The long flight to Japan ended in a frightening landing at

Tokyo Airport in thick white rain. The plane appeared to hit, rather than land on the runway, which in those days jutted out into the sea. Rab's detective afterwards confided that the steward and air-hostess had been certain that we were about to crashland.

Tokyo is certainly the ugliest city I have ever seen. The grey box-like houses which take the place of architecture are, I am told, the result of uncertainty as to their future destruction by earthquake. Rab displayed his matchless skill at a big press conference in the Embassy, which I was allowed to attend, and my usual skill at flower arranging deserted me when I was asked to do an arrangement *à la japonnaise* (Ikebana), before the TV cameras. We were invited to an audience of half an hour at their palace by the Emperor and Empress, and I had a meal sitting on the floor with Japanese ladies. I have never felt so large before or since.

On the way to the Philippines we landed at the tiny island of Okinawa, where, since it was a free port, I bought a watch very cheaply. On our return to London airport I was asked by Tom Bridges in meaning tones if I intended to declare it. 'Certainly not,' I replied, 'it's not new; I've worn it for at least forty-eight hours.' The Philippines were, I suppose, the strangest part of the world I have ever visited. At a dinner party, sitting next to a white-clad Roman Catholic Cardinal, I remarked how much I should like to visit some of the islands. 'It would be impossible,' he replied. 'There are head-hunters still living on them.'

The British Ambassador, John Addis, with whom we stayed, liked to keep his Embassy as much like the Philippine houses as possible, eschewing air-conditioning in some of the rooms. We had it in our bedroom, but not in our bathroom, into which one went as little as was physically possible. The heat was formidable. While Rab was seeing President Macapagal, I paid a visit to his wife, who was as formidable as the heat. Unaware that I was there, she entered the room in which I was waiting, saw me and beat a hasty retreat before returning to make her formal entry.

On our homeward journey the aeroplane stopped for an hour at Bangkok airport (all I am ever likely to see of Thailand), where Ebbe Munck, who was the Danish Ambassador, came to meet us, bringing me a lucky Thai charm, which he said I must always keep, as indeed I have. It was the last time I was ever to see Ebbe. Back in London Michael Hadow, one of Rab's entourage, murmured in light-hearted tones, 'Did I not hear a cheep coming from one of the red boxes?' as the customs officers met us in the VIP lounge. Since Nicko was bringing back some forbidden partridge eggs on behalf of a friend in Tokyo, this remark caused Tom Bridges to turn white with rage, but went unnoticed by the customs officials.

Almost immediately we returned I gave a dance at Carlton Gardens for William's twenty-first birthday. All the arrangements for this had been made by our friend Patricia Stewart-Bam, in my absence abroad. She had summoned a crowd of people to jump up and down on the drawing-room floor, since a ball had not been held there in living memory, to ensure that the ceiling below would not fall on to the dining-room table. The incomparable Brigadier Macnab had waved his wand to produce flowers, food and wine with his usual perfect result – though not, I must hastily add, paid for by Government hospitality.

Rab and I stayed twice at the beautiful Paris Embassy during this year with Bob and Ismene Dixon. At one dinner I sat next to M. Couve de Murville who, though he may have been pleased with Rab's powers of speaking French, made it plain that he was not pleased with the Embassy cooking. At another dinner the Dixons had invited the Duke and Duchess of Windsor. I had never met her before and was struck by her immense chic, her simple and straightforward manner, and the magnificence of her jewellery. I sat next to the Duke of Windsor at dinner and all that I can recall of this rather sad man was his saying, in a strong American accent, 'I sure hope Mr Goldwater is going to win the US elections, don't you?'

To my great credit I summoned up courage to say, 'No, sir, I can't agree.'

While staying at the Embassy, I visited Malmaison, the château outside Paris where Napoleon had lived with Josephine and where she continued to live after he left her. It was a hot summer afternoon when I wandered round this famous garden. The Empress, who loved roses, introduced and planted over two hundred varieties, from Persia and other eastern countries, which filled the air with fragrance. In the empty château a curious incident took place. I was shown round by the *gardien* and, as we stood in Napoleon's study, built in the shape of a tent, I was aware of a strong green light as though of sunlight pouring through canvas and I felt the presence of a crowd of unseen people pressing round me. I am unable to explain this vivid impression.

In July we paid our last official visit abroad when we flew to Moscow, where the kind Trevelyans, Peggy and Humphrey, gave up their bedroom in the Embassy to us. It was excessively hot with the sun beating down on the golden domes of the Kremlin, across the river from the Embassy. One evening, when it was cool, Humphrey took us for a drive round Moscow, visiting some of the churches, where he spoke in Russian to the old people clustering about the doors. The old are allowed to retain their religion. In those days the shops were empty and the ordinary people seemed uniformly sack-shaped, perhaps denied the sort of food eaten by the Intourist guides, who, by contrast, had neat figures, were smartly turned out and wore make-up. The bouquet which I presented to Madame Gromika, wife of the everlasting Foreign Minister Gromiko, had to come from Finland, since flowers in the USSR seemed to be an unnecessary luxury. I went to tea with Madame Gromika who, anxious to show her knowledge of English history, told me that Queen Elizabeth I was the mother of James I. I felt that the slight diplomatic error of putting her right was worth the historical truth. Rab and I were shown round the Kremlin, where we were obliged to see every cracked cup in the cupboard of Lenin's flat and where Rab in despair sank on to his desk for a moment's rest, from which he was seized by angry hands, outraged at the sacrilege. There was in the Kremlin an enormous and most beautifully decorated coach on display which had been sent by our Queen Elizabeth I as a present to Ivan the Terrible; I marvelled at the transport of such a vast and yet delicate equipage in those days.

Our visit to Leningrad was by train, departing from Moscow in the evening. The luxurious coach had two bedrooms and a sitting-room, and progress was by a slow, lulling speed aimed at bringing us to Leningrad in time for breakfast next day. I remember Harold Caccia's enjoyment of the astonishing meal which awaited us: sweetcakes, soft boiled eggs, brandy and vodka. We were taken for a trip on a hovercraft on the waters of the Gulf of Finland by Russian officials who were obviously proud of this, in those days, novel form of transport; we went to the Peterhof Palace, where Rab was lured in the garden under a 'tree' made of metal which spouted water when a button was pressed on whomever was below (the press much enjoyed this). We admired the beauty of Leningrad itself, but the highlight of our visit was the morning spent at the Hermitage. Not even the Uffizi, not the Prado, nor any gallery that I have seen, even in America can, in my view, rival the

Hermitage for the quality and range of the wonderful paintings it contains. Gazing at Rembrandt's *The Prodigal Son*, the Russian Ambassador from London, who was in our party, whispered in my ear, 'He was a *good* Communist.'

I have described in an earlier chapter our summer in Mull that year, when Rab spent so much of the time in London owing to troubles over Cyprus. Before leaving the Foreign Office and Nicko, I should like to quote something he wrote about Rab's dealing with the Cyprus question, and with his alleged inability to make up his mind. Nicko sums it up thus: 'He never had a head-on collision. He rarely gave a firm or final rejection of anything. He always refrained from shutting the door . . . But in bigger matters, not coming to a conclusion about a particular course of action was a positive decision. He did it deliberately and he had often found that he had avoided trouble that way.' This is not to say that when an unpopular decision was called for he would shirk it, run away from a courageous yes or no. For Nicko's words come after describing how Rab had refused to put his signature to an agreement with George Ball of the USA State Department over Cyprus, that he, Rab, did *not* agree to.

Nicko writes again:

His confidences, his indiscretions, his humour, his good temper, his imperturbability and the readiness with which he bared his soul – these qualities made Rab a very great pleasure to work for. He was also full of worldy wisdom, which, without being at all didactic, he was always ready to impart. I think I learned more in one year from Rab about political life than I did from anyone else I have served for however long.

A lovely tribute from the man who worked for him during his last year in Government. Everyone knows that the general election of October 1964 was lost by the Tories, and, though Saffron Walden returned Rab by a majority of nearly 5,000, for the first time in thirteen years he was facing life in Opposition.

9

FRESH FIELDS

On 23 December 1964 we were to travel up to Mull for the Christmas recess. Nanny and I and some of the family went to London with the luggage early in the day, leaving Rab, who had a shooting engagement in Essex, to follow later and join us for the night train to Scotland. During the morning there was a telephone call to 3 Smith Square from the Private Secretary's office at 10 Downing Street: could the Prime Minister speak to Mr Butler? I gave the telephone number of Rab's host in Essex and tried to possess my soul in patience. During the afternoon there was a second call; number 10 had failed to catch Mr Butler, where could he be found? At this I organized a hired car to meet him at Liverpool Street station and take him to Downing Street on his way to Smith Square.

I see him now when he arrived that evening, filling the front door in his big brown travelling overcoat and leading Bella, our much loved Dandie Dinmont. I could hardly wait for him to tell me the cause of the telephone calls from the Prime Minister. Harold Wilson had offered him the place of Master of Trinity College, Cambridge, a Crown appointment and the first one that Mr Wilson had made since becoming Prime Minister. The light of this tremendous news still illumines the tiny detail of Harold Wilson telling Rab how good it was to see him in country clothes. I could think of nothing else; I knew how unhappy Rab was in Opposition – his was essentially a creative nature, and the idea of opposing just for the sake of it was unattractive to him. The last time he had been in Opposition, from 1945–51, he was greatly occupied with the creation of the new Conservatism at the Research Department, but he was miserable now in George Brown's old room in the House of Commons, where it was dark and depressing, and he was trying to believe he had something to do.

Of course to leave politics was a very big step, but he was only just sixty-two years old, in vigorous health and with all the experience and wisdom which the Tories (to their everlasting loss) had rejected ready to give to this new job. With it went also the offer of a life peerage, which would still leave him a platform in the House of Lords. My heart sang at the thought of this change in his fortunes and, as we climbed into our sleepers aboard the train that night, my mind was full of what the future held.

Rab, naturally, needed time to think it over, and it was opportune that he had until early January in the relative tranquillity and isolation of Frachadil to give his thoughts to this new idea. I tried very hard not to push him towards it; all my instincts told me it was right for him, but he must feel this himself. As he walked up pheasants with Julien, who had joined us, and William, his mind was not on the few birds that Roddy drove towards us from the laurels in the Torloisk garden, but alternating between the Thames and the Cam. Eventually his decision was made and the letter which was to decide the course of our lives for the next thirteen years was posted in a country pillar-box at Gatcombe, where we were spending a weekend in January.

It was decided that the news should be kept back until after the state funeral of Sir Winston Churchill on 30 January 1965. When the announcement was made in banner headlines, it was clear that some of the journalists who wrote them regretted that this most enigmatic of political figures was stepping from the centre of one stage into the centre of another – though they would continue to write about him in their newspapers and still do twenty years later.

In February, with Rab's daughter and mine, I watched him enter the House of Lords as Lord Butler of Saffron Walden. As I sat in the gallery and heard him give the oath, and observed the complicated motions which new peers have to perform, I knew that a part of me was sad that Mr R. A. Butler, the name that had meant so much to me and to countless thousands of others, was no more.

Next month we were invited by Lord and Lady Adrian to spend a night at Trinity in the Master's Lodge. It was a daunting experience. The Adrians, who were worshipped by the college, were both of the high-thinking low-living persuasion, he as a world-famous physiologist, revered almost to the extent of Sir Isaac Newton, and she as a great philanthropist who had devoted a large part of her life to Cambridge Mental Welfare. They must have been sad at the thought of leaving their vast and glorious Lodge, but they welcomed us very kindly and gave us tea sitting on a sofa covered in grey material. Afterwards we were escorted round. The Lodge had enormous potential, but it was dark and had not been decorated for decades; it was obvious that Lady Adrian's interests were not centred on the domestic scene, since it was in need of cleaning, clearing out and cheering up.

Rab dined in Hall with the Master, and Lady Adrian gave a dinner for me in a small room which she used as a study, surrounded by filing cabinets. Two of the Fellows' wives were invited to meet me, but they both gave their undivided attention to their hostess, who sat at one end of the table with myself opposite. I took comfort in the white wine, which cheered my flagging spirits.

The surroundings in which I live have always been of enormous importance to me, and I determined that this palatial Lodge should be allowed more light and given more love. I was lucky in Carl Winter, the Director of the Fitzwilliam Museum, who was thrilled to be asked for his advice and, together with Dr Robson, we planned wallpapers and hangings suitable for the grandest and one of the oldest Lodges in Cambridge. Bob Robson was the arbiter of taste in the College, one of the few Fellows who really cared how things *looked*: years later the Junior Bursar's only question on hearing my choice for a new dining-room carpet, was 'Does Bob approve?' I also planned some modern plumbing, which the College was generous in providing. A Mr Coe, who worked there as a painter and decorator, told me later: 'I see it broke your heart when you come 'ere and see all that dirt – not fit for a lady to come to. Lord Adrian, he didn't mind it. You'll excuse my mentioning it. When we was a-taking out the old toilet seats in Trevelyan's time, the Americans offered us £50 for 'em, seeing they'd had three kings go through the Lodge sitting on them.'

The Adrians were endlessly kind to us during this transition period, he especially taking a great interest in my ideas. On my asking for white electric light switches in place of the existing black ones he demurred. 'But you won't be able to see them.' When I pointed out that you generally felt for, rather than saw, a light switch when going into a dark room, he was satisfied.

The summer passed in a flash. One of its highlights was a lunch with Princess Marina at Kensington Palace, followed by a visit with her to the Wimbledon tennis championships. I had never before travelled in one of the royal Rolls-Royces and I realized, as I sat with the Princess, that it seemed more like being in a house than a car. Rab did not endear himself to our hostess at Wimbledon. She naturally, as President, took the exciting tennis very seriously, while it was Rab's first visit there. Seated beside her in the Royal Box, she was not pleased when he murmured, 'This is not at all like the vicarage tennis to which I am accustomed.' We were not asked again.

As Rab was to write, 'The pattern of a new life is beginning to show, but the ghost of the old one is still haunting the ramparts.' But before we started this new life we decided to take a holiday. We would go to Greece. We did it in style, hiring a car to drive in the Peloponnese with a driver who was aware of Rab's fame, though he may not have known for what he was famous, and who treated us with every sort of distinction. I suppose it is impossible to put on paper one's feelings for Greece; Dilys Powell came nearest to it when she called her book about the country *An Affair of the Heart*. The feeling springs from so many sources – reverence for the myths learnt as a child, excitement at seeing household names, Olympia, Marathon, Salamis, come to life. Of all the places which we visited Mycenae was the most awe-inspiring. I never saw nature's face so loftily indifferent as in the mountains behind Mycenae; Mt Euboea is after all only 2,500 feet (lower than our own Ben More on Mull) and yet, by comparison, the Alps seem domestic. It is as though these mountains were still keeping company with Agamemnon himself and guarding secrets too terrible for twentieth-century humanity.

Approaching Delphi, the waters of the Gulf of Patras were sufficiently turbulent for Rab to seek what he called Greek courage, a glass of local brandy at the café by the quay from where we crossed by ferry with our car and driver. Across the water snow-capped Parnassos beckoned. We had decided to stay at Delphi and were rewarded by a night of unearthly beauty. Our hotel was built into the side of rock cliffs below the main street, so that the lift took us deep down to a bedroom, from where the balcony looked out over grove upon grove of olive trees stretching away to the Gulf of Corinth. Their silver leaves reflected the beams of a full moon and to complete the heavenly scene there were nightingales. Next morning, walking on the slopes of Parnassos among wild flowers and crowds of people in bright sunshine, it all seemed like a dream.

We went to Marathon, beloved of Byron, and stood on the domed mound of 192 Athenian dead, before rounding off our holiday with a week in Rhodes. Hotel guests were given charming bungalows, only inches from the Aegean, in the waters of which most of our day was spent, while every evening, we saw the sun set behind the Turkish mountains across the sea.

Back in England everything led towards Cambridge, where our new life was to start at the beginning of October 1965. Rab was installed as Master in scenes of enormous public interest. The Great Court of Trinity College was packed with spectators, while he waited outside the Great Gate for the moment when he was to knock and be admitted by Mr Edwards, the head porter, after declaring his credentials. As he waited, tall and imposing in scarlet doctor's gown, the press and public were there to photograph him. It was a warm sunny day and amongst the crowd were members of both our families watching the proceedings until, after the initial service in Chapel, we were admitted there to see the final seal set upon Rab's Mastership. Our new life had begun.

The day was crowned by an enormous dinner in Hall, where, dining with the Fellows, Rab's special guests were Edward Boyle, Geordie Selkirk, Geoffrey Lloyd and Enoch Powell, besides the male members of our family and myself. For me it was not an unfamiliar scene; August had been at Trinity and, as I looked at the painting of Henry VIII with the motto *Semper Idem* above the high table, softly illuminated by the candles below, I was reminded of August quoting those words to me on our engagement. When still an undergraduate he had taken me to tea with his Master, Sir J. J. Thomson and the terrifying Lady Thomson in the very Lodge which was to be my home. Christopher, when an undergraduate, had given me tea in his rooms (he had occupied a set on the corner of the Great Court known as Mutton-Hole Corner, where tradition says Byron also had rooms) and he was now one of the College Chaplains, while William was still here as an undergraduate. And had I not in my youth attended six successive May Weeks and six Trinity May Week Balls? But, of course, to be the Master's wife was something else.

The secretary whom Rab had engaged proved unable to fill the job and our first invitations were issued by Rab standing before me and rattling off names of undergraduates, while I feverishly endeavoured to keep pace. I soon began to realize that the familiarity which I had at first imagined wore very thin. But I loved the Lodge. Houses, like people, have personalities and that of the Master's Lodge was totally benign.

One enters from the Great Court and is immediately lapped in an atmosphere of timeless peace. The dark panelled walls of the big hall do not give an impression of gloom, but rather of a welcoming warmth, and the rather indifferent paintings of early Kings and Queens of England hanging on the walls might have been overpowering if they had been better painted. They have a primitive and rather childish style. Indeed there is nothing of special grandeur in the hall except the enormous grandfather clock given to the College by Sir Isaac Newton and dated 1708. Its tick is the heart of the house beating. Beyond the hall is the vista of Bentley's staircase – built during the first half of the eighteenth century, it is said to be able to hold ten persons abreast. I clearly recall the thunder of feet coming up it when Rab and I stood at the top welcoming what seemed like several hundred freshmen to drinks before the matriculation dinner. The first room these young men entered was the small drawing-room, which dates from 1554, and was so called, though thirty feet square, to distinguish it from the big drawing-room beyond, which, I was told, was the size of a cricket pitch. In the small drawing-room we hung the Impressionist paintings which Rab had inherited from his father-in-law, Samuel Courtauld, Sydney's father: a Monet, a Manet, a Cezanne and a Renoir. Rab was very proud of them and indeed they were the glory of the Lodge, superb paintings which were feasted on by the countless undergraduates who thronged our parties and by the Fellows of the College and their guests. Carl Winter and I had chosen a very beautiful yellow wallpaper, against which they showed to perfection.

Our thirteen years in Cambridge were Trinity's last of her centuries as a 'men only' college, and women were admitted in October 1978, four months after we had departed. But meanwhile for our undergraduate parties I always invited each man to bring a guest and naturally most of the guests were women. Rab and I regularly entertained them in the big drawing-room at noon on Sundays.

On one occasion I noticed two first-year undergraduates sitting by themselves on the floor, so I went over to ask if they were all right. 'No,' they replied, 'this is a rotten party.' I enquired what was wrong and was told 'everything'. At this I promised to bring the Master to their rooms for a return visit, when they could show us how a party should be conducted. A few days later, Rab and I climbed the steep stairs to a room at the top of New Court, where they entertained us with beer and buns in what they claimed was a proper atmosphere. I was amused to notice, however, that these same young men came happily to our parties in the Lodge after several months had passed and life in the College had won their confidence.

On one side the drawing-rooms looked out on the Great Court to the east and on to the Lodge garden with the river beyond it to the west. The ceiling was decorated with domes covered in gold leaf, decorations dating from the time of Thomas Nevile, who was appointed Master by Queen Elizabeth I in 1593. He was also responsible for the splendid fireplace in this room, which dates from about 1600. Above it the plaster decoration rises to the ceiling displaying the arms of Queen Elizabeth with the lion and the Tudor dragon, picked out in green and red and gold, and below this the College shield with on one side the arms of Nevile and on the other those of Whitgift, at one time Master and later Archbishop of Canterbury. Professor Trevelyan wrote: 'If Henry VIII founded Trinity, Nevile built it.' (It was he who built the graceful Great Court, which encloses just over two acres with buildings whose proportions are an endless satisfaction to the eye – and the equally beautiful Nevile's Court was named after him.) In this vast room hung paintings of Queen Elizabeth, Newton and the Earl of Essex, who came to Trinity as an undergraduate. It was so perfectly proportioned that, sitting together by the enormous open fire after our guests had departed, Rab and I never felt it was a big room – its space was equally adapted to contain hundreds or just us two in happy proximity. Its walls were of a thick embossed paper, which seemed to absorb sound and resulted in a harmonious buzz on a big occasion, rather than the cocktail party cacophany which makes conversation impossible.

Queen Anne knighted Sir Isaac Newton here. We know that James I, about to sign the marriage contract between his eldest son, Charles, and Henriette Marie of France, travelled from Newmarket to Cambridge telling the French ambassador to met him at the Master's Lodge at Trinity since Newmarket was too rough a place for the signing.

The atmosphere which these famous persons left behind them was totally benevolent.

If sleep was elusive sometimes, one could cross the expanses of the drawing-room's polished floor in bare feet, the embers from the fireplace perhaps still glowing and the lights from the Great Court casting shadows through the windows whose curtains we always kept drawn back. There would be lights in some of the undergraduates' windows during all the hours of darkness, and a full moon might be silvering the grass of the court and the ancient roofs. Always there would be the soft splash of the fountain, which must have soothed the countless men who had slept within the sound of its voice since Nevile erected it in 1602.

From the big drawing-room a panelled passage led to our bedroom and Rab's study as it was called. On the passage walls we hung Rab's political cartoons, originals by Giles, Vicky, Illingworth, Cummings and Low, which entranced the undergraduates, who would congregate there for hours, discussing, gazing and laughing over them.

We decided to sleep in what was known as the king's bedroom, which had in fact been used by royal visitors. This was a very beautiful large room built by Nevile and panelled by Bentley, its walls painted white, with a window to the west overlooking our garden, the river beyond and on the far side of the river St John's College, while our north window was shielded from the Fellows' bowling green by a tall beech hedge. There were suggestions of cutting this hedge lower, but on my pointing out that to the windows of St John's beyond we would be perfectly visible, the Fellows kindly desisted. There were pale pink brocade curtains already hanging at our tall windows, which went happily with the pale blue draperies of our bed to form a pretty bedroom. On the landing outside this room, from which went a tiny staircase to Rab's study, I made a sitting-room for myself. I had bookcases installed along the walls and arranged my china in an enormous shelved bookcase already there, with glass doors and an inscription over it saying, 'This case was given to the College by Sir Joseph Thomson. It contains books left by Montagu Butler'. Left by Rab's great-uncle they might have been, but they were a dark and dingy lot and I had them packed and put in the cellars for the duration, an act which caused some of the Fellows to pretend to be shocked.

Our first duty was to get to know all the members of the College, undergraduates, Fellows and their wives, partly by entertaining them and also by looking out on them from the Lodge. There was a window seat in the small drawing-room where one could sit in happy contemplation of the doings in the Great Court, at the same time learning to recognize the doers. Another help was Julia Fish, the new secretary whom Rab engaged and who became a friend of the whole family. She assisted me with card indexes of every invitation we sent out, on which I filled in as many personal details as possible to aid memory. Rab always dined in Hall on Sunday nights, and after port in the Combination Room he would bring any of the Fellows who wished into the Lodge through a communicating door. It was a great pleasure getting to know these distinguished men in this way, when they would sit chatting in the big drawing-room, drinking whisky round the fire. Their wives, who had been having Sunday supper with me, would join them in what seemed a relaxed family atmosphere. One of the wives, Barbara Hawthorne, an American, who later became a dear friend, said to my great amusement, 'You know, Mollie, Rab isn't like those old dons – he's got sex appeal.'

After they had got over the shock of a Master who was not a Trinity man (Rab had been at Pembroke College, and was elected a Fellow of Corpus Christi College before entering Parliament), the Fellows were extremely kind to us both and we soon felt at home with them. Rab, after all, had strong family connections with Trinity, since his great-uncle Montagu had been Master from 1886 until his death in 1918 and his son, Rab's cousin the historian Sir James Butler, was still a Fellow of the College. Although Rab showed scant respect for his august forebear, I think he must have shared many of Montagu's qualities; Professor Trevelyan writes that 'Butler ended his thirty years of Mastership more venerated and beloved by Trinity men, past and present, near and far, than any of his predecessors unless haply Nevile.' King George v stayed in Trinity Master's Lodge in 1912 and it is recorded that he found Dr Butler's conversation very entertaining.

One of the major pleasures of our new life was the Chapel. A few steps away from the Lodge, the building had been begun by Mary Tudor; Queen Elizabeth i had finished what Mary's death prevented, while Bentley had adorned it. Though not one of the most beautiful chapels in Cambridge, it retained a great hold on one's affections and every Sunday after Evensong I would be moved afresh by the statue of Newton in the ante-chapel, his white marble figure standing before the floodlit west wall, whereon the names of those members of the College who fell in the Second World War were written in gold. The Director of Music on our arrival was Raymond Leppard and the music we enjoyed and the singing of the choir were both equally excellent under this distinguished musician. In those days everyone, undergraduates as well as Fellows, wore white surplices and from my cushioned and panelled corner beside the Master's stall I used to admire Rab in his, for with his red hood, it suited him.

Christopher, who was a great help to Rab and me in our early days, was, of course, always there for morning and evening services; it was a personal joy to see and hear him then, though I did not often meet him, since he was busy at all hours of the day and night with the welfare of the undergraduates, by whom he was greatly loved.

And then there was Harry Williams. Harry was the Dean of Chapel, of whom I had heard much from Christopher before Trinity was part of our lives, and, though Harry says in his autobiography that Christopher had brought him to Spencers, I had been so preoccupied at the time with August's illness that I had forgotten. I had never before experienced his preaching. I use the word advisedly since to listen to Harry was a quite new experience. He was witty – people used to laugh during his sermons – he was profound and, above all, he made religion cease to be a duty and turned it into a glorious way of life in which, listening to him, you longed to share. My pen is not able to do justice to the greatness of Harry or to what I feel is his importance to the Church of England today. I can only say to those not privileged to have met him and heard him: read his books.

From the first he became and remained a wonderful friend to us, and the little that I have ever glimpsed about being a Christian I learnt from Harry during the four years that we were lucky to live under his benevolence. Church and Chapel would be packed when he was to preach. One Sunday evening I took a weekend guest to hear him at Great St Mary's. As we tore through the streets of Cambridge after a hurried dinner, she asked breathlessly, 'Why must we *run?*' and I replied, equally breathless, that it was the only way to get a seat. Harry was marvellous company and a very good raconteur who lists laziness and religion as his recreations in *Who's Who*. He had a beautiful speaking voice and I hear him now as he rose in Chapel and said, 'In the name of the Father . . .' before one of his unique sermons.

Seeing the choir on Sunday after Sunday we got to know them and they became some of our closest friends amongst the young men. The Annual Choir Dinner was always a very happy evening; much wine would be drunk and many impromptu speeches made, and when it was over we would all go back to the Lodge, where the choir, relaxed by claret, would sing Yale songs in the big drawing-room, conducted by the Organ Scholar. When Harry considered they had been with us long enough, which was never long enough for me, they trooped down the staircase and continued in the Great Court, below our windows and round the fountain, always ending with their own special rendering of 'Halleluja'.

Not long after our arrival there was a controversy about the Chapel. An idea was put forward by the Council, which met under Rab's chairmanship every Friday morning, that something should be done about the baldachin at the east end. A painting by Benjamin West of *St Michael binding Satan* had once hung there, but this had fallen from favour and had been relegated to the staircase leading up to the Wren Library, leaving an expanse of bare brown wood surmounted by an ornate pediment with rococo cherubs. Rab was asked for ideas, and passed the request on to me. I had lately seen, at an exhibition in Bond Street, some cartoons done for the new Roman Catholic cathedral in Liverpool by the painter Ceri Richards which seemed to me rather good, and I suggested his name. The Council liked the idea since they had heard of his work for St Edmund's Hall, Oxford, so an invitation was sent for him to visit us and look at the baldachin.

He eventually submitted three cartoons for the College to choose from, all of a semi-representational nature and presuming to illustrate the scene of Pentecost in gold, blue and green. They were very beautiful. Rab had them placed in the Lodge, where all could see them and pass judgement. Sir Steven Runciman, one of our Honorary Fellows, liked them so much that he offered to pay for whichever the College should choose. But how was it possible to expect 110 men to agree on a subject of aesthetics? Only a tiny percentage of this vast number of Fellows attended services in Chapel, but they were all eligible to express their views, and these were unfavourable. There are those who feel that all subsequent decoration must belong to the period in which a church or chapel was built (and the best example that I know against this view is the beautiful east window in Eton College Chapel executed by Evie Hone after the Second World War). Ceri Richards was very disappointed at losing this commission and only partly placated by my asking him to do a drawing of Rab's head.

I reflected sadly that these Fellows were the successors of those who had decided to chop Queen Victoria's bed in half. It may not have been a thing of great beauty, but its historic interest could not be denied, since the Queen and the Prince Consort had slept in it during their visit to the Master's Lodge. It is now a single bed bearing the initials V & A which the Assize Judge slept in during his visits to the College, now discontinued. The Judge, his Marshal, the High Sheriff and other worthies would process across the Great Court as far as the sundial, to the sound of the High Sheriff's trumpeters. Here they would be met by the Master and a collection of the Fellows, and all proceeded to the Lodge, where they drank mulled port in the hall. Subsequently the Judge lived in the Lodge, eating his meals in the dining-room while we ate in the hall (where he would have left his wig and gloves) and sleeping in the rooms designed for his use beneath our bedroom.

On the last Sunday of the Judge's visit he would dine in Hall, escorted by the Master with great ceremony. It so happened that on one of these Sundays Harry Williams had invited a distinguished woman theologian to preach at Evensong. Enjoying herself, she leant on the desk and gave an extended sermon, while Harry, growing desperate, watched the clock. (Hall was punctually at eight o'clock.) To the amusement of everyone Harry waved his watch; she didn't see it. Eventually, while she was still in full flood, Harry rose and announced in icy tones, 'We shall omit the last hymn, I shall pronounce the benediction from my stall and the Choir will immediately leave Chapel.'

The Judge might have said, like Louis xiv, 'J'ai failli attendre.' It has been said that I did not welcome these visits as unalloyed joy, one noble Judge even hinting to me that I had been instrumental in bringing them to an end (as if I could have done). But this was 'rumour . . . blown by surmises'. True, his staff and ours usually quarrelled over some triviality like the use of our dustbins, but I could not have quarrelled over a tradition which went back to the time of Nevile, and the College as a whole enjoyed giving hospitality to the Judge and were sad when the assizes were moved from Cambridge.

Our entertaining was made a pleasure by the help we received from our domestic staff, important members of the household. There was our faithful friend Harry, who remained with us for sixteen years in all. He came with us from Essex and was a chef whose fame was to spread throughout Cambridge. His cooking had a creative quality which dispensed with mere recipes; I would return from some grand meal in London and describe what we had eaten, and he would then produce this same dish out of his head. Once, after a luncheon at Buckingham

Palace, I told him of the first course, next day we had it at our own table and it became known as 'Palace Eggs'. It was a source of enormous confidence during great occasions to know that Harry was in the kitchen, always to be relied on.

Nolan, the butler, was an Irish Roman Catholic who looked and behaved exactly as I imagine Jeeves to have done; he was always immaculate in appearance and in his work, and no emotion showed on his face except a slight quiver at the corner of his mouth if the conversation at table became very funny. (He once allowed himself to smile as he commented, 'His Lordship would feant', when I suggested using rather large claret glasses to make up the numbers.) He had been accustomed to looking after royalty in his previous position and was thus a great help when we had visits from members of the Royal Family. Although young he had a bad heart and died, sadly in our employment. We missed him enormously and never found anyone to equal him.

Mary, our housemaid, was what the French call *inénarrable*. She had been exquisitely well trained and would talk about 'front-ways', where we lived, and 'back-ways', where the staff lived. Aristocratic looking, with an aquiline nose and perfectly permed hair and wearing a spotless white overall, she became a friend to us all and specially the college porters, to whose lodge she would slip in her spare time for a drink and, no doubt, a gossip. Our guests came to appreciate her care whenever they stayed with us, and she would take a great interest in them. ('When is that nice Lady Carrington coming again?' she would ask.) She loved the dogs and once put her head round the drawing-room door during a party to say, 'Could I have a little brandy from the drinks tray? Blackberry is having one of his fits.' The roof climbers of Trinity, who used to do the circuit of the Great Court at night, after dropping down from Hall on to the Master's Lodge, had to pass along a narrow passage outside Mary's bedroom windows when, awakened by their descent on to the tiles above her head, she would address them, minus her false teeth. 'You'll kill yourselves! I'll tell the porters about you, I will,' she would hiss. The *Trinity Review* has an article on the subject of night-climbing which states: 'Having made the safe traverse of the Master's Lodge, it is customary to observe a minute's silence on Thanksgiving Plateau above B and C staircases. It is wise to maintain the silence as we make our way to King Edward's Tower, lest we arouse our tutors from their slumbers below.'

By daylight Mary was a friend to all the undergraduates and would welcome them to our Sunday parties. As far as I knew, she only had one fault: her extreme dislike of classical music – 'Give me rock-'n'-roll.'

On one unforgettable occasion we had David Oistrakh staying with us to receive an honorary degree. He was also to give a recital in the Guildhall with the Cambridge Musical Society, conducted by David Willcocks, playing the Brahms Violin Concerto. I listened to him practising in our spare room from the landing outside. Mary was passing and I said was it not wonderful to hear him?

'No, m'lady,' replied Mary, 'it makes me feel sick!'

Oistrakh spoke little English, but his wife did and told us he was worried at what sort of performance the undergraduate solo oboist might give during the slow movement. (Perhaps he had not played with non-professionals before?) In the event he was so pleased that, during the wild applause when the concerto was over, he signalled to this young man to stand up and share in it. I was not surprised, for the serene mastery of his instrument which was displayed during this, one of the most beautiful of all Brahms' melodies, has often made me wonder if the unknown player has gone on to become a professional.

The great Oistrakh only felt able to play if he knew that his wife was waiting backstage for him – she was not allowed to come out in front. They were two most lovely people, who demonstrated how music transcends creeds and countries to unite all people of whatever political faith or none.

The Lodge was much in demand as a place for entertaining distinguished people whom the Foreign Office wished to amuse and, since we could call on college waiters to help out, this presented no difficulty. A large party of Chinese came down with their interpreter, the Dalai Lama came to a luncheon, the Sheikh of Abu Dhabi, Monsieur and Madame Schumann, for whom we gave a great dinner, and many others whose names in our visitors' book are signed in characters which I cannot define nor recognize. But, of course, the visits which caused the most excitement and pleasure were those of our own Royal family; the Queen, the Duke of Edinburgh, and Queen Elizabeth, the Queen Mother, all honoured us with a stay or a meal. The arrival of the Prince of Wales in the College must be reserved for another chapter.

10

CAMBRIDGE WATERS HURRY BY

Harold Nicolson, reflecting on the power of the senses to stimulate memory, dismisses the ear as being strong in evocation. I do not agree. I can hear now the Rolls-Royce sound, the silky smoothness of the door at the top of the staircase into the small drawing-room as it shut behind one, and equally the harsh grating noise of the door on to our back drive.

The Combination Room was separated from our small drawing-room by double doors, and the welcome sound of Rab's key as he returned from a meeting of the Council or after dining in Hall is clear to my ears today.

'Trinity's loquacious clock' in Wordsworth's words strikes the hours twice over, and its ringing every quarter of an hour just outside the Lodge windows was a worrying reminder of the passage of time as our years slipped by in this happy place. The eight weeks of the Lent term starting in January would glide away to be followed by the Easter term and all the summer festivities, culminating in May Week during June, after which there would be holidays punctuated by Rab's duties to his other universities (he was Chancellor of both Sheffield and Essex), and these would bring us round once more to October and the start of a new academic year with its challenge of unfamiliar young faces.

I had early joined the Musical Society and derived much pleasure from the College concerts. I started the tradition of Lodge concerts on a Sunday evening in the early summer. These were enormously successful with around 180 undergraduates and their guests, in Sunday suits, enjoying the excellent music which was provided in the big drawing-room. Amongst the performers were Anthony Peebles and Stephen Barlow, who both became professional musicians when they had left Trinity. After the concert was over, the audience would stack the chairs for me. This was the only occasion when the Fellows were barred, unless attending the concert, from the Master's Lodge.

During one of these functions Rab was heard to exclaim, 'It's no good going into the Lodge tonight, Mollie's got some music raging away.'

Meanwhile he was an enthusiastic supporter of the First and Third Trinity Boat Club and went regularly to the Bump Suppers, where he showed great courage amidst the crossfire of potatoes aimed by the inebriated oarsmen. He had shown the same courage at his installation as Rector of Glasgow University in the 1950s when flour and beetroots had been flung at him by the students. However, he went so far as to suggest that mashed potatoes should be served at Bump Suppers as being less painful than boiled ones. In one year's *Trinity Review* there appeared the following poem, called 'Head of the River' above the signature of a great rowing man, Dr Edward Bevan:

> The Master of Trinity, Rab,
> Is blessed with the gift of the gab
> At Bump Suppers, when able,
> He climbs on the table
> And the speeches he makes there are fab

I believe this to have been a true account of what used to happen.

But there were many and varied occasions when he had to make speeches. Tony Weir, an alarmingly clever young Fellow, and a disarmingly sweet one, wrote of him:

At the unmilitary rituals which form much of a Master's job Rab was outstandingly good. He could personalise the big occasion and dignify the small event, such as a presentation to a retiring College servant. If Adrian's speeches were thick inlaid with patines of bright gold, Rab's had the perplexing appeal of a *jolie laide*. Never at a loss for words in public, the words he found could be a surprise, and newly elected Fellows and visiting speakers were sometimes credited with unfamiliar achievements or attributes. His touch was faultless in giving recognition to those whose exertions underlay the event.

He was wonderful with the young men. He had kept his veneration for Stanley Baldwin (whose signed photograph was displayed in his study), and used to invite the members of the University Conservative Association to parties in the Lodge, where he would hold them in thrall with talk of his political life and anecdotes about Winston Churchill, whom Rab also loved, almost it sometimes seemed, against his will. He wrote of him, 'Churchill was great in everything which he undertook, as statesman, orator, writer, painter and exponent of the art of friendship.'

These young men who clustered about Rab were enchanted by his memories of the past, when he had worked with Churchill, and by the shrewdness and wisdom with which he would analyse for them the continuing political scene. This wisdom was at the disposal of any undergraduate who sought it, and many were the young men who climbed the steep stairs to his study, seeking advice on many things, perhaps an expedition to South America or how to get their theatrical venture on the road. The rowing men were not the only ones to have his support; the Magpie and Stump, the debating society, was close to his heart as was the Dryden Society, whose performances of plays he was careful to attend.

This last became a favourite of the Prince of Wales when he arrived at Trinity and proved to be a very good actor. His entrance into the College in 1967 caused an even greater stir than Rab's own, and we in the Lodge crowded on to the balcony over our front door to watch Rab greet him at the Great Gate. He drove up through cheering crowds in a Mini, and Rab and he walked across the packed Great Court before the TV cameras. Next day he made the first of many visits to the Master's study and I was allowed to come and meet him there. I remember asking him what his room was like and he confessed that it was a bit stark. He was unassuming and gentle. I asked what I should call him while he was an undergraduate and he replied, 'Call me Charles, if you like.'

Lady Longford has written:

As for Rab Butler, if he was the best Prime Minister we never had, no one could be a better mentor for a monarch he would never see enthroned. There was something beautifully apt about the situation: the Queen being called on weekly by the actual Prime Minister, and her heir calling weekly on the mighty might-have-been. On one of the visits Charles asked: 'May I join the Labour Party?' 'No,' said the Master, realising this unconstitutionalism was the result of a Marxist living on Charles' staircase.'

Prince Charles was soon absorbed into college life, where he became very popular, and could be seen bicycling round the town, or in the crowds on the banks of the Cam in company with Chris during the Bump races. I used to think, seeing him in profile in Chapel, that he bore a strong resemblance to the Princess Royal, the eldest daughter of Queen Victoria. Rab and I dined in the Prince's rooms, where the college had given him a new kitchen, in which he cooked an excellent dinner, and he also dined several times with us.

The first time he dined at the Lodge I had heard only two hours earlier that a much-loved friend, privately engaged to be married to one of my children, had been killed in a railway accident. I was almost dazed with shock and horror, but the Prince was coming to dinner and I must hide my sorrow somehow. I put him beside Rab with, on his other side, Lucia Santa Cruz, the daughter of our friends Adriana and Victor Santa Cruz, the Chilean Ambassador in London. Lucia was a most charming and accomplished girl with degrees at both Oxford and London University, whom I had invited since I thought Prince Charles would like her. Indeed he did, and their subsequent friendship was a happy example of someone on whom he could safely cut his teeth, if I may put it thus.

At another of our dinners the French Ambassador, Geoffroy de Courcel, was present and the Prince and he became absorbed in deep conversation to the frustration of some of the female guests, who longed for a word of their own with Prince Charles.

He became very fond of Dr Robson, one of his supervisors, and this fondness was mutual. When his twenty-first birthday came along, Rab and I offered to vacate the Lodge to enable him to give his own party there, but instead we were invited with other members of the College to the celebrations at Buckingham Palace. This was an unforgettable event, consisting of a reception, followed by a concert in the ballroom and afterwards a magnificent supper party at which the guests sat at little round tables in the happiest and most carefree atmosphere.

Some months later I met Lord Plunket, who had made many of the arrangements, and he told me how they had been growing the flowering shrubs and the flowers which adorned the Palace that night for months in anticipation. He said what pleasure he had taken in seeking out young and amusing people to fill the party for the Prince, and in arranging the seating at the supper tables to give the maximum of enjoyment to everyone. Rab and I enjoyed ourselves hugely.

It was a great satisfaction to him that the Prince, in spite of all the interruptions to his studies, social and public, and a term spent at Aberystwyth, managed his degree so well, getting a 2/1 in Archaeology and Anthropology, and a 2/2 in History.

During his time with us I sensed that under his gentle and sometimes hesitant approach, there was a strain of toughness which would be invaluable to him in years to come.

In 1968 Christopher's five years as Chaplain were over and he left us to become Chaplain at the London Hospital in Whitechapel. It was a great sadness to me to lose him. As I helped him move into his tiny flat behind the hospital, I reflected on the enormous change in his surroundings, from the perhaps privileged ambience of Trinity College to the 700 sick beds of the impoverished but lively and vital East End of London. He became as integral a part of the hospital as he had been of the college, where he was extremely popular and his farewell party in the Old Kitchens (which had been transformed into a place for gatherings of all kinds) was a very big affair at which the undergraduates presented him with a carriage clock. His last appearance at Evensong was deeply moving. Harry Williams came into the Lodge as soon as the service was over to praise Chris's sermon; he had been as much inspired by it as Rab and I. In his autobiography some years later, Harry paid Chris a tribute: 'In my experience,' he wrote, 'from 1938 to 1968 Trinity never had a better Chaplain than Chris.' I know that I should offend Chris's Christian humility were I to write of all the goodness he shed around him.

Harry himself left us the following year to become a monk with the Community of the Resurrection at Mirfield in Yorkshire, but not before he had given us endless fun; the undergraduates sang at their annual revue 'Let's get drunk with Harry the monk.' Chapel was never again quite the same for me without those two.

Harry took part in the Proust dinner which I gave one summer. This consisted of those, and only those, who had read *A la recherche du temps perdu* all through, and thus even Rab was debarred until the coffee and liqueurs. Harry came dressed as a Roman Catholic priest, complete with biretta, to the exquisite astonishment of all those who saw him crossing the Great Court thus arrayed. A young Fellow who was an aficionado of the great Marcel helped me with the menu, where everything was related to the novel, for example Steak Putbus accompanied by *pommes sautées* Prince Von; we tried to find the least known characters after whom to christen our dishes. Proust's biographer, George Painter, and his wife came down from London to crown the evening with success, though they were the only ones not dressed for the part. I decided to go as a combination of Madame Verdurin and myself. After it was over, I received the following limerick:

111

A sodomite student who used
To read nothing but Housman and Proust
When invited to tea
By Blank, Staircase E
Murmured, 'If I'm seduced I'm seduced.'

which was handed to Chris after dinner in Hall by a very respectable and outwardly staid Fellow, Professor Broad, with the request: 'Just give this to your mother for me.'

One of the disadvantages of living in Cambridge was the lack of country walks. We would put our dogs in the car and drive out to the Huntingdon road, turning off at a public house called The Trinity Foot (the name referred to the Beagling Club) to the villages of Swavesey and Over, where we walked along the sodden and rather sad banks of the river Ouse as it wound its way through the fens to Ely. Or we might drive towards Grantchester and walk through its meadows beside the Cam, but this way we were always within sight of houses; the scenes described by Rupert Brooke in 'The Old Vicarage, Grantchester' had long been built over. But although we lived in a town, there were owls hooting on the Backs, tree-creepers on the college trees and always in summer the serene and lovely notes of a blackbird echoing round the Great Court. Our dogs were forbidden by college rules and had to live with us as cats. ('I heard your cat barking away,' one of the Fellows was to remark.) On one occasion I returned from a shopping expedition in the town, greatly laden, with Susie's poodle Blackberry on a lead. At the Great Gate I stopped, putting the dog in a basket to carry him across the Great Court. I was seen by the courteous Dr Kitson Clark, who hurried gallantly forward to help, innocent of my burden. Although he said nothing, he must have been horrified to find himself holding one handle of a basket containing the illicit Blackberry.

The Fellows of the College were a constant source of amusement and pleasure to us. A charming and very distinguished mathematician, Professor Littlewood, was passionately fond of music, and on discovering that I had gramophone records of his favourite Beethoven, the last Quartets, he came every Sunday evening to listen to them. He was also very fond of whisky and Rab usually had to escort him back to his rooms after everyone else had gone home to bed. I said one evening that I was surprised he did not have his own gramophone since he derived so much pleasure from mine.

'Oh,' said Professor Littlewood, 'I never thought of that.'

Next day he spent several hundred pounds in Cambridge buying the latest equipment and records. A tiny old man, he was also an ardent rock climber. One night at port in the Combination Room Rab found himself alone with Jack Littlewood, sitting in total silence. The manciple (as the butler is called at Trinity) bent over and whispered in Rab's ear, 'Try rock climbing, my Lord.'

Mr Simpson, another of the Fellows, had occupied the same rooms in the Great Court since 1911. His was a restless figure in Chapel since he would change his seat several times during a service, where he would be clad in shawls and scarves over his surplice and hood. He moved about Cambridge with a pair of secateurs, constantly snipping at bushes or shrubs, to the annoyance of other colleges. I once saw him cutting his own very thick grey hair out of his window overlooking Trinity Street. There was a story of a motor car which had knocked him over and thereby sustained damage, while Mr Simpson was unhurt. He would bring wine and spirit into meals in Hall contained in medicine bottles. His great enemy for some long-forgotten reason was Mr Gow, known to generations of Eton boys, where he had taught, as 'Granny Gow'. He would sit in a chair placed in the sunniest part of the Great Court for hours on end and complain that tourists would constantly come up to him, always with the same questions: 'Where is Prince Charles's room?' 'Where is the toilet?' I once passed with a bunch of lillies of the valley from our garden in my hand.

'Where are you taking those flowers?' he demanded rather crossly.

'To Mr Simpson,' I replied.

'Do nothing of the kind, he is not worthy of them. Give them to me,' was his rejoinder.

In 1972 Professor Gallagher returned to Cambridge from Balliol College, Oxford, as Harmsworth Professor of Imperial and Naval History, and succeeded the dear Professor Patrick Duff as Vice-Master of Trinity. Jack Gallagher, a witty Irishman and brilliant lecturer (Julien, when an undergraduate, has spoken of how his lectures would lift a subject far above the realms of ordinary thought and speech) became our friend immediately and was an enormous help to Rab in college affairs. Like Rab, he had a nose which could sniff out trouble on the horizon. Two of his intimates, Anil Seal and Tony Weir, were also ours, and they formed an important and formidable trio.

The Master's appointment ends at the age of seventy, but the Fellows can, if they wish, reappoint him until the age of seventy-five and, when Rab reached seventy in December 1972, it was Jack Gallagher who early the next year organized his re-election. This was a very great joy to both Rab and me since were so happy at Cambridge. It was also rewarding to be wanted. Rab wrote: 'Jack Gallagher exceeded in assiduity any sheepdog in rounding up the flock' to vote for this welcome outcome, and we were very touched to get a letter, now framed, from the whole college staff expressing their pleasure at the extension.

A visit which was unwelcome to me was paid by Mr Macmillan, who came to attend, with Rab and Lord Adrian, a debate at the Cambridge Union. True to my vow, I refused to have him in the Lodge and he was housed in the Judge's rooms, but came up to drink whisky with Rab in his study.

'Where is Mollie?' he asked.

Rab replied untruthfully, 'She is in bed with a cold.'

It was, therefore, unfortunate that the taxi which had been ordered to take them all to the Union headquarters failed to turn up. Rab, somewhat flustered, appeared in the small drawing-room appealing for me to drive them in our car, which with a very ill grace I was forced to do.

We usually went twice a term to Gatcombe, a house in Gloucestershire which had been left to Rab in the 1940s, of which he was very fond. (He was an example of the adage, 'A sense of possession turns all into gold'.) Since Friday mornings were given over to the Council, we were obliged to make the three-hour journey in the afternoon, driving across country on narrow and crowded roads much used by heavy lorries. We were often driven by Julia Fish, who would bring us back by the same tiresome and tortuous route in time for Evensong in Chapel on Sunday. These glimpses of the country were a joy to Rab who loved the farm and his sheep and the endless talks with his farm manager, but to me, beautiful though I found Gatcombe, it was a flawed house. Too big for us to be able to make convenient or comfortable, it had endless drawbacks which I believe were all rectified when Rab sold it to the Queen as a home for Princess Anne in 1976.

I was told that when the Duke of Edinburgh was being shown over

Gatcombe he remarked, 'The Butlers can only have picknicked here,' and picnic we certainly did.

The exotic smell of the datura in the eighteenth-century conservatory is one of my happiest recollections of the place. I am very pleased to think that there are young people and children living there now who will certainly have changed the atmosphere: as I have said, houses have personalities, and on one occasion when I had been unable to accompany Rab, he telephoned me in the evening saying, 'I don't feel easy here on my own.'

Every summer we made our way to Mull for six weeks, staying a night in the Border country with Steven Runciman on the way. Steven was not only a good friend to Trinity, he was ours as well and stayed with us in the Lodge for all the college feasts. His castle at Lockerbie was an enjoyable *asile* after a five-hour drive from Cambridge. Here, at Elshieshields, he did his own cooking, refusing all offers of help and washing up between each course of the excellent dinner he provided. Afterwards, we would sit in the tower-room and, beside a log fire, Steven would ennumerate details of the various ghostly happenings which his guests had experienced. Rab and I were never quite sure how much he believed them himself.

Another yearly visit which we paid was to Oxford in June for the Christ Church gaudy feast, staying in the Deanery of this sister college to Trinity. Our first visit happened to be on 24 June, and there was something romantic and exciting about looking out on to the very garden, and seeing the very door which Alice in Wonderland had gone through on this warm midsummer night. The astonishing beauty of the Christ Church library in Peckwater quad and the melodious boom of Big Tom's bell were all new and exciting introductions into this, to me, unknown university, which wore a sophisticated face compared to our own dear Cambridge.

Rab had a very low threshold of boredom, which he was generally able politely to conceal, but at one Honorary Degree Ceremony in another college he became impatient with the interim for drinks before lunch, standing in a hot garden, and wandered off to find somewhere to sit in peace. When the meal was announced, I went in search of him and to my astonishment found him serenely reclining in his resplendent red gown upon a conveniently closed seat of a water-closet, surveying the scene through its open door in a relaxed and thoughtful manner. If the conversation at any of our dinner parties was not up to his standard, he would start to improvise, provoking gales of laughter from his neighbours at the table. Afterwards, as I led the ladies to the drawing-room, they would say: 'Your husband has been telling us such funny stories about you.' These proved to be inventions which I had to treat with the greatest discretion.

Amongst the few things which he could not do well was to drive a car. An amusing incident arose from this when he had taken Peter Carrington, who was then Minister of Defence, and Geoffroy de Courcel to shoot with Julien at the latter's farm thirty miles from Cambridge. The road was a narrow, twisting one through the Cambridgeshire and Essex lanes, and Rab had apparently driven mostly looking over his shoulder to talk to Peter in the back of the car. When I arrived later with Iona Carrington and the lunch (Julien's wife Paddy and I took it in turn to provide shooting lunches), Peter, the bravest and most gallant of men, approached with a stern face and said, 'Mollie, you must arrange for someone else to drive back – Geoffroy and I can't have Rab do it again, it's too terrifying.' Rab was enormously proud of his new Volvo car and it was difficult to persuade him to let Peter's detective have the pleasure of trying it out. In the end they all arrived back thoroughly shaken since the detective's driving had been worse than Rab's.

He could, on occasion, have a marvellously impervious manner, which was of infinite value. We were giving a large and rather formal dinner in the Lodge when, as the assembled guests politely sipped and talked, the butler announced in ringing tones, 'The Vice-Chancellor and Lady so-and-so.' I had totally forgotten I had invited them, but, as I handed them over to Rab, not a muscle of his face moved, while I flew to tell the kitchen and to rearrange the seating in the dining-room. I found Harry, in his white coat beside the kitchen table like a surgeon about to operate, and owing to his skill all went well. Afterwards Rab said, 'You had a surprise tonight, didn't you?'

We had kept on our London home, where we went in the middle of every week during term, giving our staff a rest and seeing our friends. One visit I will not easily forget. I had left the house early after breakfast and met Rab for lunch at one of his clubs, the Carlton. Seated at a table for two by the window, after giving our order to the waiter, he said, 'I think you ought to see this,' and pulled a letter from his breast pocket. It was from the Queen's Secretary, Michael Adeane, and contained the Queen's offer to Rab of the Garter. Sitting at that table I burst into tears; I was so overcome with joy. (I believe this is a quite normal reaction since the wives of other Knights of the Garter have told me that they did exactly the same on hearing this news.) It was lovely to feel that all Rab's years of service were to be rewarded with this highest order of knighthood.

The investiture of a new Knight of the Garter is an affair which seems to come, as it should, from the distant past. The Knights and their wives assemble in a beautiful little chamber which, I believe, was created in Windsor Castle by George IV specially for this purpose. Here the Sovereign in her own Garter robes invests them. I was fascinated by the ease and deftness with which the Queen fastened their sashes and placed the collar around their necks, while one of their supporters, of which each new Knight has two, holds the actual Garter round the new Knight's left leg. It is amusing, since the Knights are by no means in their first youth, to hear them swearing their oaths to fight loyally for their Queen in language which suggests the jousting of a tournament in the Middle Ages. One of Rab's supporters had severe arthritis and found placing the Garter, when he had to kneel down, quite an ordeal. (I believe this part of the ceremony is now performed by Lord Abergavenny, the Chancellor.) The Prelate of the Order is by custom the Bishop of Winchester, and in 1971 he was none other than our friend Falkner Allison, who had married us when Bishop of Chelmsford, and who now said the prayers.

After this most touching and impressive ceremony came a sumptuous luncheon in the Waterloo Chamber. New Knights are seated very high at this banquet, and Rab was placed next to the Queen Mother, while I had the pleasure of sitting next to the Prince of Wales. Every successive year we sat nearer the bottom of this enormous table, though always in most distinguished company and I cherish the memory of lunching next to Lord Longford, Lord Rhodes, and my old friend Launcelot Fleming, when he was Dean of Windsor. The procession to St George's Chapel afterwards was quite literally a wash-out since the rain was so heavy and continuous that it was cancelled, and we were driven down from the castle in motor cars. This was a small tragedy for those of our family who were standing on the grass to see us go by, but once inside the chapel for the service the scene was enthralling. The organ pealed, the trumpeters

117

trumpeted, the Royal Family were there looking splendid and the singing of the choir made the blood run cold with its beauty. The Knights in their stalls, wearing their velvet robes of 'heavenly blue', as the colour is described in the investiture service, stood beneath their brilliantly coloured banners, while more colour was provided by the heralds dressed like figures from a pack of cards, and the various uniforms, red, blue and gold. I suppose there is not a piece of pageantry anywhere to equal it.

Beneath the pomp of this occasion there runs a vein of domestic pleasure which stems from the perfect manners of the royal servants, from the moment when a liveried footman opens the car door at the entrance to the castle. It is as though all the chivalry we are about to celebrate in prayers and hymns has been transformed into the handing of a dish or of a drink upon a salver.

Soon after this, we dined in London with Raymond Leppard, whose increasing engagements as conductor and performer all over the world had made it impossible for him to continue as our Director of Music. John Betjeman was also at the dinner and talked of Rab's Garter, speculating as to why Lord Longford had at the same time been made a Garter Knight. I reminded him of the crusade against pornography which he had just undertaken.

'Of course,' cried John gleefully, 'Frank got it for purity.'

It was a happy thought when the College put two new stained glass windows in Hall, one with Lord Adrian's coat of arms and the other with Rab's, which last bore the motto of the Garter, *Honi soit qui mal y pense*, traditionally the words of Edward III, whose arms are incorporated in the flag that floats above the Great Gate, since Trinity College can trace its faint and far beginnings to the benefactions of this king.

11

PACIFIC SKIES

Rab gave the Romanes Lecture in the Sheldonian Theatre in Oxford in 1967 on 'The Difficult Act of Autobiography' before a distinguished audience, including many friends. He spread his palette with colourful names from whom he quoted and drew his conclusions; Marcus Aurelius, Virginia and Leonard Woolf, Gibbon, Montaigne, Harold Nicolson, Pepys and many others.

'Portrait painting,' he said, 'is difficult enough. But the self-portrait, whether through the medium of a mirror or a book, is even more so,' and, quoting Dr Johnson, 'No man but a blockhead ever wrote except for money.' Rab suggested that this is perhaps a reason behind many autobiographies, but, in a long quotation from Chateaubriand, he gave other motives such as books born of boredom in retirement. He asked why there have not been more women autobiographers, and commented that 'women are shrewder observers of others than themselves'. It was a splendid and stimulating talk. I disagreed with only one thing he said: 'The stigma of many autobiographers, talking at inordinate length about the ordinary details of life', since to another generation the ordinary details can become fascinating revelations. He gave the palm to Rousseau, but asked if you must describe your physical and emotional life 'as Rousseau does – the variety of countesses you have lived with, if you are to get a first class in the final School of Autobiography? If so, the outlook for many of us is grim and puts recent Prime Ministers, with their solemn records of public transactions, in the shade.'

The lecture's success was partly due to Rab's skill and long experience as a public speaker, but also because of his chosen subject. He had been thinking for some time about writing his own auto-biography, and decided to seek the help of Peter Goldman, disciple and polymath, who now came often to the Lodge from London. He would arrive with his Jack Russell terrier, Jimmy, firmly attached to him by a piece of string, and he and Rab would be closeted in the study, from which could be heard much laughter. He was an old friend whom Rab could trust to guide his words into a literary shape, since he himself was more of an orator than a writer.

Evelyn Waugh has said somewhere that, whereas a writer thinks in words, a politician thinks in sentences, and indeed rereading Rab's letters I have noticed how little of himself comes through. I had also found, when going through with him something that he had written for a speech, that his ear was unable to detect when he had used the same word three times in as many lines – the sort of thing that doesn't matter when spoken, but which can jar on the printed page. But he was brilliant at constructing a speech from uncoordinated jottings submitted by the different departments of whichever Ministry he happened to be at the head of, and they had been fascinated in the Foreign Office to watch him spreading out all the bits of paper on the big conference table in the Foreign Secretary's room and, with a pair of scissors and many pins, putting together the final draft. 'It was an amusing and instructive experience,' observed Nicko Henderson.

Thus, with Peter Goldman's help emerged a classic, *The Art of the Possible*, which was published in 1971 to enormous acclaim. If the Fellows of Trinity did not seem exactly excited about it, the reviewers were ecstatic. Some of them rewrote his life in the process, respectfully praising the Education Act, celebrating his triumph with the 1952 Budget and delighting in the Churchill stories. Nearly all speculated on why he had not become Prime Minister.

Ronald Butt wrote in *The Times*: 'Lord Butler has done the trick in 274 pages of beautifully printed prose in a book which has momentum but no *longueurs*. It is rivetingly anecdotal: it is frank in revealing his own persona and is, for much of the time, intentionally very funny.'

Enoch Powell wrote in the *Daily Telegraph*: 'Among recent autobiographies and reminiscences of public men, Lord Butler's Memoirs, published today, are in a class by themselves. In literary distinction, choiceness of expression, polish and balance, they make the rest look like botchwork.'

The *Guardian* published an interview between Rab and Terry Coleman, entitled 'The Impossible Lord Butler', which was very funny and ended with Rab saying, 'I don't at all resent what Wilson [Sir Harold] said about trying for the impossible. After all, Julius Caesar, whose career as a youth was probably the most dramatic in history – my God, he was always going for the impossible.'

Almost the most poignant piece came from Derek Marks of the *Daily Express*, who had been one of the waiting journalists outside the house on that January night in 1957, when Rab had not, contrary to expectation, been sent for by the Queen. He wrote:

For his dignity and good humour that night I personally can vouch. At midnight he invited me and two of my *Daily Express* colleagues to have a drink in his home at Smith Square. For a man who had just been pipped to the Premiership his invitation took some beating. "Whatever are you doing here at this time of night? What terrible lives you chaps have, come in and have a drink." Nobody could have failed to admire to the utmost his manner and bearing.

And so on. The *Financial Times*, the *Observer*, *The Listener*, every national newspaper and most of the provincial ones sang his praises. The book was reviewed in India, Canada, the USA, and Rhodesia; it was translated into Spanish, it may have been translated into Chinese for all I know, and the first edition sold out within a week. It left many questions unanswered – maybe that was part of its fascination. I greatly liked Woodrow Wyatt's tribute: 'This is a book without pomposity or boring self-justification. It is imbued with the cultured and balanced appreciation of an ancient Athenian. Whatever he is dealing with – his early life, India, Munich, education – he is urbane, intelligent and worthwhile.' Rab himself was delighted by Roy Jenkins's writing that the volume 'fully justifies his position as President of the Royal Society of Literature'.

The American edition carried an introduction by Professor J. K. Galbraith, who wrote it from Cambridge, Massachusetts; in it he said:

Uniquely among autobiographers, English or American, he writes to rejoice the reader and not himself . . . the humour has importance beyond the book. It is one of the much debated mysteries of British politics why Rab Butler never became Prime Minister, for he was in competition with markedly less able men. Partly the answer, one cannot doubt, is here. He could never view himself with the terrible solemnity of the truly determined politician. And the determined men, for their part, are always a little suspicious of those who are amused. So it is the solemn men who make it.

While we were at Cambridge, Rab gave many lectures, received many honorary degrees, and for this purpose we made many journeys overseas. But one of the first lectures he gave was at the Senate House in Cambridge, the inaugural Nehru Memorial Lecture. Lord Mountbatten brought his two daughters and dined afterwards in Hall at Trinity, and I realized then, sitting next to him, what a beautiful voice he had, cajoling, caressing and unexpected. Nehru had been at Trinity when a young man and his family and Rab's had strong connections of friendship in the past; Rab was the obvious choice to deliver this lecture, and I, who am totally ignorant of all things Indian, found it one of the most interesting I had ever heard him give.

I did not go with him to Calgary, Alberta (from where he returned with a white cowboy hat as well as his honorary degree) since I funked the two air trips, there and back, within the space of only five days. In 1967 we went to Zürich for the first Winston Churchill Memorial Lecture, which Rab delivered at the University of Zürich. His title was 'Churchill's Personality and Europe', and he wove a fascinating picture of world policies before our entry into Europe, quoting Jean Monnet, who said in 1950, '*Les anglais ne croirent qu'au fait. Créez le fait européen et ils y croirent.*' He described Churchill's outlook on the international scene as sweeping and spacious, hence his speech in Zürich in 1946 with its 'magnificent appeal for a United States of Europe. The Zürich speech has fine language in it but for language let us look at one of his greatest and his nearly-last debating speech in the House of Commons in March 1955, after his eightieth year, when he held a packed house in silence while he expounded his appreciation of the world situation which had determined the Government to press forward with the manufacture of the hydrogen bomb. In its deterrent power he founded his hopes for peace. "It might well be," he said, "that by a process of sublime irony, we have reached a stage in this story when safety will be the sturdy child of terror and survival the twin brother of annihilation." '

Rab gave a talk on education in Paris to a large audience. I only remember of this the excellence of his French and the abominable accent in which he spoke it. (*Ecoles* rhymed with souls.) But he was to keep the Anglo-French connection very much alive by holding a colloquy at Trinity, in March 1968, to which came Christopher Soames from his Embassy in Paris, the editor of *Le Monde* and many other distinguished personalities, both French and English, to air their views on all matters of common concern to the two nations. If Rab spoke the language of Racine, Christopher Soames spoke the most marvellous and modern French slang.

Our journey to South Africa in 1969, for Rab to give the Chancellor's Lecture at Witwatersrand University, was fraught with drama. He was unaccustomed to booking his own air passages and we were to fly to the Canary Islands by the first line which had come into his head, which happened to be Iberia. Our faithful Julia Fish drove us to Heathrow, where she and Susie meant to see us off. After a long wait in the VIP lounge a Spanish official came with many regrets and shruggings of his shoulders to tell us that our plane was still in Spain – but never fear there was another one. After a further delay he was back, he regretted infinitely the second plane had failed to turn up. There was nothing for it but to have dinner in the airport restaurant and go home to bed. Next morning Julia drove us, to Gatwick, where there was a British plane to take us to the Canarys in time to catch our ship. Julia was an excellent driver but, alas, the road to Gatwick was unfamiliar, the early morning traffic was heavy and, as we pushed our way slowly through it, tension in the car built up. No one spoke except Rab, who repeatedly commented, 'We shall never do it.' However, we reached Gatwick before the plane left and climbed thankfully aboard. Our troubles were not over; there was a strong head wind, and it became clear that we should miss the ship. Rab consulted with the pilot, who sent a radio message to the *Edinburgh Castle*, where Captain Dryden agreed to put off sailing for two hours. We were whisked, unsearched, through customs at Las Palmas, bundled into a taxi, and finally boarded the ship via the luggage gangway while rows of outraged passengers looked down over the rail. It had been a near thing.

The *Edinburgh Castle* was charmingly old-fashioned with chintz curtains to our stateroom portholes, and mahogany furniture. We had asked for a table to ourselves in the restaurant, and the only people we knew on board were my cousin Malcolm Napier and his recently married wife, Mariota Murray. We met every day, the only people to enjoy it, in the ship's swimming-pool, where the waters slopped and heaved against the side following the movements of the ship. On deck at night it was wonderful to watch the gentle swaying of the ship's funnel and mast against the stars, and listen to the faint hum of the soft night airs in her rigging.

After this delicious ten-day interval the harsh contrast of South Africa was very striking. After our visits to Central Africa, where one met the black man and woman on equal terms, it was hateful to witness the inhuman treatment meted out to them by the Afrikaners. The Africans would squat in the gutter, not allowed to sit on public seats. But worse, far worse, was the fact that the impoverished Africans must pay for their children to go to school, while the white child was educated free.

Dining with members of the Government in Cape Town, and being escorted round Stellenbosch University, one was not struck by any extraordinary merit in these 'white' people. It was a relief to visit Cape Town University, where the charming Sir Richard and Lady Luyt invited us to a luncheon; we had met them both in Central Africa and he was now the enlightened Vice-Chancellor of this University. Rab gave a short talk to the students, which was listened to with a touching avidity, and many were the questions which he dealt with in his usual inimitable manner afterwards.

Even better was our arrival in Johannesburg, where we stayed with the Vice-Chancellor of Witwatersrand University, Professor Bozzoli, known to everyone as Bozz, and his wife Cora, who instantly became our friends. Here Rab was to give his lecture on 'Academic Freedom', and here we saw that academic freedom was indeed a reality, thanks to Bozz and his freedom-loving students, and Cora and her 'black-sash' ladies. No two greater enemies of apartheid existed than the Bozzolis. It was a most interesting time. We were taken, wearing white overalls and helmets, down a goldmine and saw a gold-pour. We also saw the pathetic living quarters of the black miners, who were not allowed to bring their wives and children with them. The Afrikaner overseer told me of an 'amazing development': an African worker had been injured in the mine and a white man had actually given him mouth-to-mouth resuscitation – this was considered an event of quite heroic proportions. We went to Soweto, peopled by children and the old during the day until in the evening, as we saw, the train-load of workers returned from Johannesburg, where they were forbidden to live, many of them clinging to the outside of the train. We went to the trial of Lawrence Gandar, editor of the *Rand Daily Mail*, who had been arrested for publishing descriptions of conditions in African prisons, and who was being cross-questioned in a tiny courtroom where, strangely, the Royal Arms were still in place above the Judge's seat. He was a Mr Justice Cillie, a political judge, who interfered whenever Mr Gandar's counsel spoke, while giving free rein to the prosecuting counsel. There was a large body of Africans at the back of the court, vociferous in their support of the defendant.

William Rees-Mogg, at that time editor of *The Times*, had gallantly flown from England to testify for Lawrence Gandar, to whom we spoke during an interval of the trial. He said he expected to be found guilty and to lose his passport in consequence. He was indeed found guilty, but the trial had caused such worldwide interest that the South African authorities dared not confiscate his passport.

The Bozzolis took us in a tiny aircraft to stay at a game reserve called Mala Mala. We slept in thatched rondavels while, from across the river, came the night-noises of animals: screechings of monkeys, anonymous grunts and an occasional roar. Next day in an open Land-Rover we visited these animals, elephants, giraffe, rhinos, lions, zebras, and the little bushpigs whose name I do not know and who trot about with their tails in the air. We were driven by a white game warden, and a black one sat in the back, armed with a rifle.

We followed rough tracks through thick, low bushes and sparse trees, occasionally leaving the track to get closer to the animals. Once we backed quite sharply from a herd of elephants. It was an entrancing morning, trespassing on the animals' own territory.

On the evening of 8 April, Rab delivered his lecture. He gave it in the big hall of the University, following a ceremony when the Vice-Chancellor invested him with yet one more Honorary Degree. (When Rab, as Chancellor of Essex University, conferred an honorary degree on Harold Wilson, I asked Mary Wilson how many of these her husband had received. When she replied thirteen, I could not resist telling her that Rab had fourteen.)

His next lecture took place the following year in India, where we stayed in conditions of immense luxury at the President's palace in Delhi. This vast Lutyens building, conceived for the Viceroy, gave Rab great pleasure. We had what seemed an army of people to look after us, and at breakfast I had only to raise the coffeepot to pour out a cup before I was pounced on, the pot snatched away and the coffee solicitously poured for me. Rab was greeted every morning by one of the President's three equerries dressed in naval, military or airforce uniform of immaculate drill, which looked no different from our own, and we were both touched to hear the band playing familiar marches when the guard was changed and, morning and evening, the army bugle calls of Reveille and Last Post.

Miss Gandhi invited us to visit her in the Parliament building and seemed nervous and tense. Was it far-fetched to remember that her aunt, Mr Nehru's sister, Madame Pandit, had been a friend of ours while High Commissioner in London? They were not on good terms.

We laid a wreath on Gandhi's tomb and drove through flourishing fields of short-stalked grain crops to Agra, where we saw the Taj Mahal and the Red Fort. We were lucky to see this shrine to a loved wife of long ago by the light of a full moon. Someone said, 'Look at it through the gate house where a hanging lamp swings – the Taj itself will appear to float and swing', and indeed it did. Rab's lecture to the Indian Council for Cultural Relations was called 'Survival depends on Higher Education', and was followed with breathless interest by a vast audience. I will only quote one sentence: 'I would like to state that your country and any country would be wise to allow the education budget to be level with even the defence budget.'

From India we flew to Canberra, where the difference was startling: India so ancient, swarming and pullulating with people; Australia by contrast so empty and so young. The change from the overzealous care of our attendants in the President's palace to the university flat which was put at our disposal, was comic. Here the fridge was stocked and we were left to get on with it in true free-and-easy Australian style. Rab had been invited to lecture at the University of Canberra by the family of Arthur Yencken, an Australian who had been a member of the British Foreign Service and a friend of his. His widow was our hostess and drove us from Canberra to her home near Melbourne, thence to Victoria and finally to Sydney. Rab gave two lectures on successive days on 'Problems of Diplomacy, Past and Present'. The subject seemed old-fashioned here in this vigorous, striving, emerging country – emerging in the sense of an upsurge of talent in every branch of the arts and sciences. He was listened to politely, but as never before I felt that what he said was out of place. The ethos of Australia seemed very concerned with its own enormous potential which, driving through its vastnesses, one was made much aware of. A country that could turn a river round and make it flow the other way, as they did the Snowy river, might not care too much about the niceties of diplomacy.

In Sydney we met Stephen, on his way to take up a job with the Bush

Brotherhood, teaching at a school in Northern Queensland. He had already worked in voluntary organizations in India, Ceylon and Rhodesia and, making friends in all these countries, could be described as a citizen of the world, although he felt most at home in France and spoke excellent French. On this occasion he had found Sydney, where he arrived two days before us, with not a room to spare because of the Queen's impending visit, and had to squeeze into a hotel far above his price. He resolved to go without food until we arrived, since he was short of money, and we were met by a skeleton who had survived two days on drinking water. He soon returned to normal staying with us in the Wentworth Hotel.

From Sydney we flew home via Hong Kong and I shall never forget my first landing at an airport where I was to go many times in future years. It was sunset, and the crimson sky was reflected in the equally crimson waters of the harbour, from which the surrounding islands rose in dramatic dark shapes.

We returned to Hong Kong in 1976, this time for Rab to open a new science block at the Chinese University. He had requested some information about what to say before going there, and the Chinese Vice-Chancellor, Professor Lee, sent him a speech of such excellence that Rab delivered it, word for word as the Professor had written it. On this occasion we stayed at Government House with Sir Murray and Lady Maclehose. I am indebted to Mr Alan Reid, a director of the Hong Kong firm of Matheson, for the information that this colossal building was put up by the Japanese for their own governor during their occupation in 1941–5. It was of an indeterminate architecture, – a mixture of a palace and a barracks with towers and balconies; spacious and comfortable inside. Rab and I had a room four times the size of our bedroom at the Lodge, with an equally large dressing-room, a sitting-room and two bathrooms. Lady Maclehose made us extremely comfortable.

Our last journey from Cambridge was to listen and look, rather than for Rab to lecture; we went on a Swan's Hellenic cruise. The visit to Olympia was something never to be forgotten; was Coleridge's Alph, the sacred river, the Alpheus of this magical place? We went there on an April evening; the ground was covered in wild flowers and the soft rays of a setting sun haloed the bushes in gold and fell on the stone columns and trunks of the pine trees, whose resinous scent filled the air. We gathered round a lecturer, a beautiful Greek woman, who told us in faultless English the purpose of these ancient games. The competitive spirit which obtained a thousand years ago has been softened by the centuries, so that to the modern visitor Olympia presents an atmosphere of indescribable peace and harmony. At Ephesus, the present Bishop of Durham, the Revd David Jenkins, read to us from the Acts of the Apostles, chapter XIX, which describes the riot which took place there. Sitting in the open-air theatre we heard every word he spoke. Rab and Anthony Powell, the writer and also a passenger on the cruise, were photographed together, standing beside a noticeboard which announced in Greek and English that this was all that remained of the Ephesian brothel.

At Patmos we rode on mules to the supposed site of St John the Divine's retreat, and crossed in a storm to Crete. Here Rab managed to catch a chill which threatened to be disastrous. In an agony of anxiety, I watched the other passengers go ashore at Delos, thinking of the ship's doctor's words: 'He is only a step away from pneumonia.' He lay in our stuffy little cabin, which I only dared visit every so often, since I feared to use up the oxygen; the porthole would not open. On deck the peaceful beauty of sea and islands were a cruelty to my mind. Next day the cruise ended in Athens where, to my infinite relief, an ambulance came to the dockside to take him to the Evangelismus Hospital while I followed in a taxi. He had a lovely room with views of Hymettus and Salamis, but of what use were these when the nursing was primitive? The language barrier was also total: I had to draw a picture of a teapot and cup to indicate that he wanted tea. But there was an excellent English-speaking doctor who took him in hand, and he gradually recovered, while I stayed nearby in the Embassy.

But while we journeyed about the world, time had not stood still at Cambridge, and I began to count the months remaining to us in the Lodge. As I pushed my nose into the lilacs in the Fellows' garden, I would think, 'Next year I shall be smelling them for the last time.' There were so many 'last times' to everything we did. At Christmas, after everyone had gone to bed, I went back to the big drawing-room by firelight, trying to impress on my memory for ever the wonderful Christmas tree reaching to the ceiling and sparkling in the half dark.

In January 1977 the Duke of Edinburgh had been elected Chancellor of the University, and this summer he came to Trinity, where he was now an Honorary Fellow, for a garden party given in his honour. A small marquee was put up in Nevile's Court, and here the Fellows waited to receive him. As Rab and I crossed the grass towards it with the Duke and his detective, Rab discovered that the latter had once been his own detective and they fell to discussing old times, and in doing so lagged behind the Duke, who reached the marquee with only me beside him. My heart sank; the duty of introducing the Fellows had fallen on to my unready shoulders, but a merciful providence prompted my memory and their names came pat. The Duke stayed in the Lodge later in the year and delighted us by being such a charming, easy guest. The Lodge was grand, but it was not exactly Buckingham Palace, though in thanking us afterwards the Duke told us how much at home he had felt.

That last year fled away until the month of June 1978, with all its farewells, stared us in the face. It was wonderful weather and we went often to Spencers, which Rab had bought back from Julien for our retirement, to swim in the pool. Rab was in splendid form that term, full of wit and gaiety, so that all said, 'Master, are you then pleased to be leaving us?' But the truth was that we were going to miss them bitterly, Jack and John, Denis, Ralph and Pat, Bob, Tony and Anil: their name was legion. All the dear familiar faces and places were gradually slipping into the past. A great happiness, in the midst of all the goodbyes, was the marriage of Christopher, which took place that June, to a clever young doctor from the London Hospital. Elizabeth had been at Girton, and came down to Cambridge to receive her Doctor's degree in the Senate House that month, staying in the Lodge where we gave a party for them both.

The College was infinitely generous with goodbye parties, from the undergraduates who fêted us with individual invitations to an enormous party in the Fellows' garden to which every undergraduate was asked, and it was so hot that the champagne corks popped over the trees; the college staff gave their own party for us, and finally there was a great farewell dinner in Hall when Rab delighted everyone in his speech by saying he would rather have been at Trinity than continue his political career. Harry Williams's place as Dean had been taken by John Robinson, the distinguished author of *Honest to God*, which he wrote while Bishop of Woolwich. During our last Sunday morning service we were all touched when he made a little farewell speech, bidding us of the Lodge goodbye. He began with Julia, went on to Susie (who came frequently from London for weekends) and finished with Rab and me.

One of my last memories of life in the Lodge is of the sound of Rab going through his books in his study and throwing those he wanted to dispose of on the floor – thud, thud, thud.

The move back to Spencers was going to be not only melancholy but also demoralizing, with all one's possessions in disarray; I suggested to Rab that he might spend a week in a health farm in Suffolk, where he would be comfortably looked after, while Julia and I got on with the move.

The last night came, and next day I drove him to Shrublands, when, coming back without him to the empty Lodge, I was seized with a mood of great and unaccountable sadness.

12

AU SOIR À LA
CHANDELLE

Spencers welcomed us back. The lime trees on the lawn were still in
flower and their heavenly smell filled the air and flowed in at the open
windows. Rab loved the trees round the house and the oaks which grew
in the park – his special pride was a pre-Armada oak which took five
adults, with arms outstretched, to span the trunk. It was a pleasure to
our country-bred ears to hear the sound of summer leaves, which had
been missing in Cambridge. Also in our ears were all the good wishes we
had brought from there, from Fellows, young men and College staff
alike, wishing us a happy retirement, to which we now looked forward.

The Times printed an article headed 'Cambridge without a Butler:
like a master without a servant.' Beneath it the centre page piece began:

The departure of Lord Butler from the Master's Lodge of Trinity College,
Cambridge, this month closes a chapter in a remarkable family history. The
Butlers have maintained a consecutive tradition at Cambridge as dons since
1794. The last three generations of the family have produced at least 12 fellows
at Oxbridge colleges, among them three professors. Lord Butler's father and
great-uncle were, like him, heads of Cambridge Colleges. No other family can
claim such a galaxy of academic stars. As Lord Butler puts it, "The Keynes
and the Darwins may have the edge on us in intellectual brilliance, but in terms
of the number of fellowships, there is no doubt that we win."

Above this piece of potted family history was a photo of Rab looking
slightly battered, but ineffably himself.

Prowling round his new home he was pleased to find how well our
things fitted in and to see his books unpacked and ranged on his library
shelves, while the paintings were hung exactly where he would have
wished them to be. (He used to complain: 'None of my own works are
thought fit for the public rooms,' but this was not true since several were

on the walls at Spencers.) He had been quoted by the press, talking of retirement, as saying, 'When we look out of our windows we shall see only cows', and indeed he now acquired a small herd of bullocks to eat the grass with which we were surrounded, and delight his heart; he was extremely fond of cattle. Julien negotiated the buying and transporting of these for him since Richard Butler, his eldest son, like Julien a nearby farmer, was now President of the National Farmers' Union and too busy for these transactions. Rab was proud of the knighthood conferred on Richard, while he much enjoyed talking to both him and Julien on farming matters, a subject close to his heart. Much has been made, of his alleged inability to make up his mind; Lord Carrington has said that he liked to try an idea, like a suit of clothes, and wear it for a little before deciding one way or another, but on the decision to come back to Spencers he had no doubts – it was I who demurred until I had discovered that the house had no 'ghosts' from the past and was entirely neutral and prepared for happiness. When Rab said that he found it more beautiful than Gatcombe, my cup was full.

But this state of affairs was not to last long. A routine visit to a doctor in Cambridge only two weeks after we had settled in disclosed that all was not well with Rab: there were polyps in his intestines which must be investigated.

I remember looking at the desk at which the doctor sat in a state of shocked unbelief. Rab was immortal; the ills that flesh was heir to could not touch him in any positive way, and yet, driving away from the doctor's door together, the aspect of the whole world had changed in one half hour.

Mr Everett performed his investigation a month later and, while it was taking place, I waited at Spencers in a state of what can only be described as breathless anxiety. The words are often used but were, that afternoon, the only ones to convey what I felt. As I waited, Mr Holman, who had been our keeper when August was alive, came to call. He was on holiday and had come to look at his old shoot, now run by Julien and another keeper. It was an enormous strain to appear interested in his talk of how many pheasants they reared at his present post in Norfolk, the prospects of the coming season and such matters, while all my thoughts were on the operating table.

At last the telephone rang to tell me the exploring of Rab's abdomen was over, he was well and I might come to fetch him tomorrow. But there was not much relief in being told we could go away to Mull and enjoy our holiday since an operation would be necessary on our return. However, we went to Frachadil and gradually its healing powers dimmed the edge of apprehension, while the remembered pleasures of hills and sea, of walks and swimming filled the days, until a fresh terror entered our lives. Again it was a routine visit from the local doctor, called in because Rab had a chill I wanted to banish, which disclosed that his heart was fibrillating, a new word to me; beating unevenly. Frantic telephoning to our doctor in Cambridge confirmed that this was something new; his heart had shown no irregularities during the recent investigation. Troubles never come singly and it seemed the end of the world, on our journey home, to find that our chauffeur, requested to meet us at the Station Hotel in Glasgow, had failed to turn up. He was supposed to drive the heavily-laden Volvo home, since the doctor had said that Rab must go by train rather than drive all that distance.

The hotel security man recognized Rab and, seeing our obvious dismay at being thus deserted, came to our rescue with offers of help in finding a driver. The only cheerful moment during this episode occurred when I went in search of water for our Jack Russell terrier and found Elizabeth Home seated in the hotel with, resourceful woman that she was, a dog's water bowl in her hand-luggage. When we arrived in London, there was our ever-faithful Julia to meet the train; she had heard of the unexpected departure of the couple engaged to look after us at Spencers and came to drive us back there. Rab was able to enjoy the beauty of his home in spite of what lay before him, the hospital and all that it entailed, but every time he extolled an aspect of it a knife turned in my heart. I had read, I think in Keats's letters, that none enjoy the beauty of the world like those about to leave it. These cowardly thoughts I kept to myself as we wandered about the autumn fields and park, and I remembered a doctor in the South of France who, summoned because Rab had a sore throat, had said to me, '*Il est toujours si bien moralement.*' When the time came for him to go into Addenbrookes Hospital, I took a room in the University Arms hotel, with Jack our dog, to be nearby. I will remember forever the two days I spent in an agony of mind, walking Jack round the fields at the back of the hospital, while the London trains passed and repassed on their everyday travels to Cambridge. How true are Auden's words in 'Musée des Beaux Arts': 'About suffering they were never wrong,/ The Old Masters: how well they understood/its human position: how it takes place/while someone else is eating, or opening a window, or just walking dully along.'

When those endless days were over and the surgeon told me that they had not, after all, had to perform the major surgery that was feared, a weight almost impossible to bear rolled away. Later I thought of the French doctor's words again as I watched Rab's calm, unmoved face while Mr Everett disclosed that they had found, and removed, traces of malignancy. The joy of driving him back to the University Arms, of the gins and tonics in our room before dining together, of going peacefully to bed in the hotel bedroom, was beyond description. I even forgave Jack when, drifting off to sleep, his whining told me he wished to go out, and I took him down in the lift and past those in the lounge in my nightclothes, out onto the grass of Parker's Piece.

We went home to Spencers next day rejoicing when Perina left her job at John Sandoe's bookshop for a week to cook for us, since we were still without help. From then on life gradually returned to normal. We celebrated Rab's seventy-sixth birthday at the beginning of December with Helen and Michael Adeane, who came for the weekend. Though Rab had given up shooting himself, he took Michael to shoot with Richard, and at teatime Tony Weir came from Trinity with a vast birthday cake for the ex-Master, while in the evening we gave a family dinner party, our first since he had come out of hospital. But there were setbacks. Returning from a visit to his dentist in London, I wrote in my diary, 'Is Rab euphoric?' And I was worried because he seemed confused and forgetful, unsteady in his gait, while Richard's wife Sue, lunching at Spencers on Christmas Day, found him less well than he had been two weeks earlier at Richard's shoot. William and his family, on holiday from Hong Kong, were spending Christmas with us, and it was he and Julien who put their fingers on the trouble.

'Who,' they asked, 'is responsible for Rab's drugs?'

Research disclosed that Rab had told the doctors at Addenbrookes he was used to taking a certain sedative – one that I took very occasionally for stress, and he had once tried and fancied it would be good for him. None of the doctors or our own GP knew who had prescribed it, but all took Rab's word and it had built up in his system over the weeks, producing the symptoms which had alarmed us all. It was stopped immediately with good results. In spite of this hiccup, he was able to enjoy Christmas with small doses of the large party of both our families assembled round him.

In February we went away to St Mawes in Cornwall for two weeks. I was still sufficiently anxious about his heart to try to avoid the little hills with which it is surrounded, and if on our walks the road was too steep, I would summon a dear man who worked at the hotel to bring his car and drive us up it. In March Rab was able to travel to London, and we went to a dinner in the House of Commons given for us by Robert Rhodes James, Willie Whitelaw, Francis Pym, Ian Gilmour and Rab's MP son Adam. (Rab's second son, Adam, had been elected in 1970 as Conservative MP for Bosworth, delighting Rab by beating a Labour candidate, Woodrow Wyatt, and increasing his majority with every successive election.) Next day we returned to Cambridge, to Trinity, and received a great welcome at the Commemoration Feast. We stayed in the Lodge with our successors, Sir Alan and Lady Hodgkin; it was a strange experience to be there in a spare room.

Our friend and GP Dr Veater came regularly to see Rab and there were trips to Cambridge for him to be checked by Mr Everett, but mercifully they both found his health improving. By April he was so much his old self that he went to a luncheon given by the *Evening News* at the Royal Festival Hall, where he discussed with Melvyn Bragg and others the forthcoming general election. The full-page spread which the newspaper gave to this function described Rab: 'The shrewdest and wisest of the veterans who had known the Prime Minister, Mr Callaghan, and Mrs Thatcher, leader of the Opposition, since they were political babies.' They quoted him: 'Mollie says I am a very good speaker, but I could not do what Mrs Thatcher does. The impressive thing is that she does it at all.' On Election night, 3 May, we went to two parties, first at the BBC, where everyone was convinced that Labour would be returned again, and then at ten o'clock to Barton Street in Westminster, where Pam Berry was holding her usual election night party, which was, sadly, her last.

This witty hostess, with her black velvet eyes and distinctive voice, gave parties of enormous *éclat*, and this was no exception. Her house buzzed with excited talk that night as her guests, MPs, journalists both English and American, writers, academics, wits and the *beau monde* gathered round the television sets in every room or sat at the tables spread with marvellous food and drink. The returns came thick and fast, and excitement mounted as it appeared that we might be going to have a woman Prime Minister for the first time. Rab and I, enjoying ourselves vastly, stayed till 3 a.m.

Soon after this return to power of a very different Conservative Party from the one he had been used to, Rab again took up his habit of attending Grillions Club which he always enjoyed. I see him now, coming back to our flat in Whitehall Court after one of those dinners. I would hear his key, then the front door would bang and he would be standing just inside it, waiting for me to help him off with his overcoat, while he murmured, 'They put me in the chair.' They always did, and I have been told by other members of this exclusive dining club how much everyone relished his indiscretions while he held the table with his talk. Grillions always elected the Prime Minister of the day and there was discussion about whether to extend an invitation to Mrs Thatcher. I believe they did, and that she, most discreetly, never attended. I would take myself over the river to the Festival Hall whenever a concert coincided with a Grillions evening. It was one of my greatest pleasures to sit, ideally in the company of 1,999 others, enjoying music. The ordered beauty of the orchestra, the movements of bows on violins and cellos, the elegance of the black and white picture they made, were a perfect accompaniment to the joy of listening. Seeing a great conductor in charge of supreme music brings Hamlet's words to mind: 'What a piece of work is a man.'

Back at home we spent much time in the swimming-pool, planted more roses and shrubs in the garden, and picked up the threads of our Essex friendships, seeing much of Julien and his family, to whom Rab was devoted. Gradually the rhythm of life returned to normal with regular visits to London, staying at our flat from where we went to Windsor for the garter ceremony, and to a great ball at the American Embassy given by the Annenbergs. An enormous 'room' made of glass with a dance floor had been put up on the lawn behind the house, its roof and walls hung with flowers which had been flown from our host's home in Florida. I thought sadly that the flight had caused them to wilt. A humbler task which Rab performed for the first time in his life this summer was to shell some peas for me during a gap in our domestic régime. In early July we returned to Mull, taking Julia with us, and flew south at the end of the month to dine at 10 Downing Street, where Mrs Thatcher was giving a seventieth-birthday dinner for Peter Thorneycroft and his wife. Rab was by now so energetic that, our flat being just off Whitehall, he decided we would walk to the party and, though I was wearing my best dress of palest Chinese silk, walk we did, being overtaken by the Homes, who offered us a lift which Rab stoutly declined. For nothing less than a dinner with the Prime Minister would he have interrupted our stay in Mull, and here we returned by train next day. Christopher sailed in *Duet* from the south to join us.

It was the summer of the terrible weather at sea which caused disaster to so many yachts in the Fastnet race and, listening to accounts of this on the wireless with Chris's wife Elizabeth, we were thankful when he telephoned from Northern Ireland, where he had been persuaded to put in by his crew. Soon afterwards he brought *Duet* into Tobermory harbour, and all on board came to Frachadil for hot baths and a dinner of venison, to which twelve sat down. Though they made light of the storms through which they had come, it must have been a welcome change.

Rab was preoccupied this August writing a lecture he was to give at the Metropolitan Museum in New York later in the year. He had been invited to give the second of the Sotheby Parke Bernet Lectures and chose as his subject 'An Amateur's Life with Art and Artists'. He was helped in this by Susie, who was reading English Literature at Birkbeck College. She sent him Tolstoy's *What is Art?*, Oscar Wilde's *Decay of Lying* and Iris Murdoch's *The Fire and the Sun*. He made much use of the last named, which tells us 'why Plato banished the artists'. I was flattered when he included three paragraphs from Proust which I pointed out to him. He ended with one of them: 'But excuses have no place in art and intentions count for nothing: at every moment the artist has to listen to his instinct, and it is this that makes art the most real of all things, the most austere school of life, the true last judgement.'

Our visit to the USA took place in mid-November; we flew in Concorde, thus fulfilling one of my ardent ambitions and had the experience, which only travellers in that gallant aircraft know, of arriving at Kennedy Airport an hour before we had left Heathrow. Maybe people are by now so used to flying faster than sound that they think nothing of it, but, when the pilot announced that we were doing so, my eyes ridiculously filled with tears. Rab had been Chairman of the Home Affairs Committee in the House of Commons, which agreed the go-ahead of Concorde; whether the pilot knew this or not, he invited

Rab up to the cockpit for the landing after only three and a half hours' flying time.

We stayed at our favourite Carlyle Hotel as the guests of Sotheby's. We felt very much on the spree as we breathed the invigorating New York air, prowled round the Metropolitan and Frick Museums, and lunched with Nin Ryan and John Pope-Hennessy. Michael Stewart had come from Sotheby's in London with his wife Damaris for this occasion, and Peter Wilson, the famous auctioneer with his velvet voice was there too. The Lecture was held in a hall at the Metropolitan, which in spite of its size was full. In the audience was Nicko Henderson, now our Ambassador in Washington. Amongst his opening remarks Rab said: 'In a technological society in which material plenty is matched by spiritual starvation, they [the arts] remind us of the existence of a higher order of values and of further heights to which the human spirit can be elevated.' It was not the most polished talk I had heard him give, but it was one of the most human, and was greatly enjoyed.

Next day we flew to Washington to stay at the British Embassy with Nicko and Mary Henderson. They were entertaining the American press at dinner that night and Mary had laid on a very English dinner in their honour (not quite Cottage Pie, but not far from it). Afterwards, as I sat talking happily in their drawing-room to Mr Carter-Brown the young director of the Museum of Modern Art, it all seemed very different from my terrifying encounter in that same room with Rose Kennedy, of fifteen years before. On that previous visit there had not been time to explore Washington, but now Rab and I were driven along the Potomac, saw the Arlington Cemetery, the statue of Lincoln, the Washington Monument and, best of all, the Gallery of Modern Art. Our return home by Concorde allowed us to leave New York in the morning, and arrive in London in the early evening, feeling fresh enough to change at our flat and attend the Queen's Diplomatic party at Buckingham Palace that night. It was fun saying to the friends we met there, 'We were in New York this morning.'

On 2 December there appeared in the *Sunday Times* Atticus column an interview which Rab gave to John Mortimer. Mr Mortimer says:

In search of the old, humane, heart of the Conservative Party, I rang the bell of a cavernous Whitehall flat and Lord Butler, stooping a little at 77 [he was exactly a week short of it] came out of the shadows. "You'd like a little whisky?" he said. "My wife's not here and she said I mustn't make tea. I've never really got the hang of boiling a kettle."

This remark of Rab's was caused by my fear of his electrocuting himself, since it was true that he had never boiled a kettle. I regretted very much having to miss this interview, which proved to be a light-hearted affair.

Later that month we were invited to visit Mr and Mrs Thatcher at Chequers, where an almost Dickensian atmosphere of pre-Christmas cheer prevailed. I was placed beside Denis Thatcher at lunch and tried to forget that I had ever read his supposed letters in *Private Eye*, while Rab, next to our hostess, felt that all his well-aimed and well-meant shots missed their target.

Although we admired her many virtues, Margaret Thatcher was not our favourite political character. She seemed to lack a sense of humour. When Alan Haslehurst was fighting the seat at Saffron Walden at a by-election, Rab and she met in the cattle market to support the candidate. The following week we were with the Thatchers at a party in London. 'I bought that black bull we saw for you, Margaret,' murmured Rab. The look of stunned horror on her face was almost pathetic.

The year 1980 was to bring Rab's last big political speech. He was extremely worried by the Government's new Education Bill, of which Clause 23 proposed that parents would have to pay for their children's transport to school. This was a direct volte-face of the provisions in his 1944 Education Act, and he had received literally hundreds of letters from angry parents from every part of England, Scotland and Wales to protest, and beg for his help.

Rab and the Duke of Norfolk, who also got many letters from Roman Catholic parents, formed a holy alliance to combat Clause 23.

Rab's first speech in the House of Lords devoted to this cause was on 25 February, when he began,

My Lords, I rise with some emotion to speak on this subject, since I have not had occasion to make either critical or positive observations on the 1944 Act practically since it was passed . . . I am afraid I shall not have the agreement of all my noble friends, or necessarily the agreement of any part of the House, when I criticize certain portions of the Bill . . . With regard to transport, I find this matter very contentious . . . The reorganization of primary education in some rural districts has been based on the belief that there will be free school transport.

He spoke for nearly half an hour and his speech made a great impact, though not such a great one as his second speech on 13 March. That afternoon, after the Duke of Norfolk had opened the debate, Rab rose at 3.52 p.m. to make the last major speech of his career. Anne Norfolk and I sat among the peeresses, hanging on every word that was spoken in a chamber which, for packed excitement, rivalled the House of Commons. Rab was listened to with deep attention. He had spoken of Winston's hold on the Commons in his eightieth year, but Rab's own at seventy-eight was immensely inspiring. 'Politics,' he said, 'is not all intellect; politics is largely a matter of the heart and people are feeling this deeply all over the country . . .' The House loved it. The Duchess and I could hardly refrain from cheering when, at 6.26 p.m., voting had taken place and our husbands had won, beating the Government by 104 votes. After it was over we went for a drink and, finding the bar crowded out, moved into the House of Commons. Here Bertie Denham, Chief Whip in the Lords and an old friend, found us and said, 'Not only do you not vote with us, you don't drink with us.' Next day there was a banner headline in the *Daily Mail*: 'School Bus Defeat for Maggie' – but it was not to defeat the Government that Rab had rebelled, but to save the promises of his Act.

All that beautiful summer of 1980 Rab and I lived a normal life together; we gave dinner parties in our flat, he went regularly to Grillions, we lunched with the Norfolks, we dined with Frank and Kitty Giles, we spent several weekends with Geoffrey Lloyd at Leeds Castle, during one of which Peter Walker, then Minister of Agriculture, came to open the new vineyard. At the yearly Garter luncheon at Windsor the charming footman, carrying drinks down the line of guests in the wake of the Queen, murmured of Rab, 'Looks a lot better than last year – must have a good doctor.'

I replied, 'What about a good wife?'

'Oh, yes, m'lady,' was the response, 'every time I see you I wish I was twenty years younger.'

Rab presided as usual at the degree ceremony at Essex University and made two wonderful speeches, during the morning and afternoon sessions, and we swam constantly in the pool at Spencers. It was our last carefree summer.

The visit to Mull in August was as halcyon as ever until, on 24 September, the first cloud, no bigger than a man's hand, appeared on our happy horizon. Going to bed that night Rab had a pain in his arm. I rang the Mull doctor, who pooh-poohed my fears. At midnight Rab was suddenly sick and I again rang the doctor, who came, gave him an injection and said his heart was 'all over the place'. Next day he came early and found Rab's heart had settled down, and said that we might travel south as planned provided he made no effort on the journey. As our taxi drove us from Oban to catch the sleeper train from Crianlarich that night I looked at the darkening mountains, fear clutching my heart, and wondered if we should ever see them together again. We never did.

There followed a nightmare week at Spencers. Rab got no better and, on 2 October, Dr Veater pronounced the dread word 'hospital'. I went in the ambulance with him to Papworth and waited with him for what seemed an eternity until a young houseman came and started being efficient. I pleaded that Rab was so tired, could this treatment not wait till tomorrow? I shall never forget his reply: 'Your husband is in heart failure.'

When I eventually left, the road to Cambridge was unfamiliar, and at the University Arms Hotel everyone had gone to bed, but a dear doorman who knew me produced a sandwich and the half bottle of champagne which Rab, in the midst of his own trouble, had told me to order.

This was the first step on the road of Rab's declining health along which I was to walk beside him, sometimes in hope and at others in despair, yet always with the same certainty of his immortality. I have been told that my confidence was a bonus to our states of mind, since we were so close that Rab would have been bound to pick up any loss of hope on my part. His own pluck and fortitude during the eighteen months that were left were everything I had come to know in him: '*Moralement il est toujours si bien.*' The fortnight he spent in Papworth was almost a happy one, since he started to get better immediately and I was able to be with him from 9.30 in the morning until seven in the evening, allowed by the busy nurses to do small tasks for him ('the best unpaid nurse on Cardiac', they said), and reading to him when he wished or just sitting quietly chatting. I would eat my lunch in the hospital canteen and make myself scarce while he had his afternoon sleep. Driving back to Cambridge at night, when my Mini ploughed through the splash thrown up by the lorries which passed me, it was wonderful to know that he was in such dedicated hands.

Rab came home from hospital on 17 October, but was confined to the ground floor. A bed was put in his library and a 'baby alarm' fixed from there to our room so that he could call out for me in the night. I would go to sleep listening to the sound of his breathing.

Later that month, on our twenty-first wedding anniversary, our doctor gave us the good news that he found, for the first time, an improvement. I had never kept a diary beyond recording appointments and the movements of husband and children, but ironically, now that life had contracted to one room and ventures out to the garden if the weather was clement, I found the days filled with details of pulse, blood pressure, pills, sleep or lack of it. Rab had always enjoyed talking to William, finding his conversation stimulating, and I ventured to ask him and Caroline for one night's stay, since they were briefly in England. During this evening I find in my diary that we were all convulsed with laughter and fascinated, listening to Rab talking on the telephone to Ian Waller, political editor of the *Sunday Telegraph*, about Suez, Macmillan and Eden; his illness had not diminished his touch.

Amazingly he recovered enough to want to go to London and the Queen's Diplomatic party at the end of November. We spent two nights at the flat, where from our windows high above St James's Park I remember being moved by the mysterious beauty of the sunset. As I helped him to dress in black silk stockings, knee-breeches and tails, he said, 'Pull the Garter tighter.' I did so and the gold buckle came away from the blue velvet. Consternation! But by good fortune there was in the flat one of those curved safety pins used for babies' nappies – a relic of some visiting grandchild – with which I was able to make a surprisingly good job of securing this important decoration round Rab's leg. He looked splendid and we set off to the visitors' entrance at the Palace, where there was a lift to take him up to the Picture Gallery. Here he was greeted by many friends – Quintin Hailsham, the Pallisers, Lord and Lady Denning, the Caccias, Prince Georg of Denmark, the Carringtons, the Norfolks, the Robert Armstrongs, the Archbishop of Canterbury and Mrs Runcie, who endeared herself to me by saying, 'I believe you're Christopher's mother', and many others.

During the evening I found myself sitting beside Hugh Grafton and, glancing at his gartered leg, saw that his was even more ill-fastened than Rab's. I offered to retie it for him. 'Don't touch it,' he said, 'the buckle broke off while I was dressing and it's done up with a nappy-pin . . .'

By eleven o'clock Rab had had enough and we found that one of the charming Palace servants had already called for our car to save him waiting. He was tired but triumphant on going to bed. He even managed a night at Grillions and on return the doctor found his pulse, chest and blood pressure had not suffered. But, alas, he was trying too hard to get back into life, and a visit by car from Spencers to Claridges, for him to give prizes at a luncheon given by the Wolfson Foundation, tired him greatly. It was terrifying to hear him give two short speeches which were obviously an effort. In spite of every care at home, these various excitements had tried his heart and once more we made the journey to Papworth. This time I led the way in my Mini, weeping for my poor Rab as I drove. Once again his wonderful heart specialist Dr Hugh Fleming and his assistant Dr Turnbull did the trick and he improved, but, as we watched the ominous sunset from his room in the hospital on the last night of 1980, I wondered what 1981 would bring.

EPILOGUE

Those who write of imaginary characters can put down as much as they wish about them: they can be as tender or as indifferent as they choose. Where the subject is real, perhaps the most real person on earth, there are inhibitions. In describing Rab's last months I could not, nor do I seek to, pluck out the heart of his mystery, but just to re-live the time together as it slipped away.

Anxiety is a stratified state of mind. There is the immediate sense of terror, blacking out all reason, which will cause the anxious one to clutch at the slightest word or sign to relieve itself of the overwhelming sensation of fear. And there is the strange fact that the self is so anchored, deep down, to the certainty of the loved one's permanence that it cannot yet comprehend disaster, in the way that a storm causes the waves to rage on the surface while on the seabed all is calm. It was thus that I existed from hour to hour during this time.

The year 1981 was to bring sorrow and joy, according to the changes in Rab's health, which fluctuated much. It was to bring a third visit to Papworth, and the arrival of a succession of night nurses at Spencers to supplement my care during the days. ('D'you realize you've been out of the room for a quarter of an hour?' he was to ask me somewhat accusingly once. I took it as a great compliment.) We had invested in an electric chair called a Range Rover which gave him freedom and enormous pleasure. He would buzz about the garden in it, often going over the edges of the grass paths into a border, from which he would need to be pulled, or sit beside me on its comfortable seat while I sprayed the roses or cut off their dead heads. Sometimes he would bump over the rough grass in the park to inspect his cherished cattle, who would cluster round him, blowing out the sweet smelling breath from their moist nostrils as they viewed this strange object. During the summer he sat for his portrait to a young artist, Margaret Foreman, who

144

had won a prize at the National Portrait Gallery and with it a commission to paint the gallery's chosen figure: Rab. He decided to wear evening dress with the sash of the Garter, black and white and blue, for this picture, and Margaret held her sittings in the drawing-room with the open French window behind him. She sewed threads into the carpet round his feet to be certain of getting the exact position each day. Between sittings Rab and I would stroll on the lawn in the sun – he most bizarrely clad for the garden in mid-morning.

This was also the year when he started to write again; he had secured the help of an editor the previous autumn who came many times to Spencers to discuss this book. *The Art of Memory* consists of nine essays, profiles of people he had known and wanted to write about: Nehru, Walter Monckton, Ernest Bevin, Halifax, Chips Channon, Aneurin Bevan, Iain Macleod, his cousin the poet Charles Sorley, and a long passage on William Temple and educational reform.

Writing *The Art of Memory* was a great interest to him, and led to his reading many more poems of both World Wars, which he had not done before. He was particularly moved by those of Wilfred Owen. Charles Sorley was killed aged twenty in the First World War, and this, plus the fact that he, like Rab, had been at school at Marlborough, and that some of his poems were about their school, influenced Rab greatly. He had often quoted to me lines from Sorley's 'Expectaus Expectavi':

> This sanctuary of my soul
> Unwitting I keep white and whole,
> Unlatched and lit, if Thou should'st care
> To enter or to tarry there.

Looking back on Rab's own life I feel there is a particular appropriateness in the last three lines of the poem:

> Thy servant stands, call Thou early,
> Call Thou late,
> To Thy great service dedicate.

It has been set to music as an anthem, which I was to choose for Rab's service in Westminster Abbey. The beautiful melody, which has a special poignancy for me, was sung most wonderfully by the Abbey choir.

W. F. Deedes (now Lord Deedes) reviewing the book for the *Daily Telegraph*, pays special attention to the 'Sorley and Midst the War Poets' chapter. But first he reflects back to the 1963 struggle: 'His patrician nature, his pride in service, the whole bent of character rendered a fight for himself improbable – no, impossible . . . We get a different glimpse of this complicated man in the tribute he includes in this book to his cousin, Charles Sorley, one of the less-noticed poets of the First World War.' He quotes 'Spring Offensive' by Wilfred Owen, saying: 'Few will have read it, and as it affected Rab so strongly it is worth giving in full':

> Halted against the shade of a last hill,
> They fed, and lying easy, were at ease
> And, finding comfortable chests and knees
> Carelessly slept. But many there stood still
> To face the stark blank sky beyond the ridge,
> Knowing their feet had come to the end of the world.
> Marvelling they stood, and watched the long grass swirled
> By the May breeze, murmurous with wasp and midge,
> For though the summer oozed into their veins
> Like an injected drug for their bodies' pains,
> Sharp on their soul hung the imminent lines of grass,
> Fearfully flashed the sky's mysterious glass.

'Almost more than I can bear,' Rab wrote of this poem. Bill Deedes's review is very perceptive. He knew and loved Rab well, he knew the poet in him and the warrior. Denied the chance of serving in either world war (he was too young for the first and his injured arm would have prevented the second), he writes of him as 'always conscious of having missed the privilege of wearing uniform', and goes on to describe 'the tormenting struggle that went on in this man, most rare in politics: the reluctant surrender of personal success to some other distant call'.

Ferdinand Mount wrote in the *Sunday Times*:

These modest pages are a comforting reminder that civilized, attentive, recognizable human politicans do exist . . . What comes out here are qualities of temperament rather than mind – principally patience, decency and cheerfulness. Like Baldwin he brought with him none of those Celtic mists which so frequently fog our affairs.

And David Wood, Rab's friend for so many years as a Lobby Correspondent, and now just retired as political editor of *The Times*, praises him in these words:

We shall not see the like of Rab Butler again in public life. I say it at a venture, yet with confidence. Here stood a man who served as proof that a first-class mind can live in politics against second-class minds . . . Anybody who has served in post-war politics, in any role, has come under his influence, no matter what their party.

Nearly all the reviewers referred to what David Wood called 'a few faults [of editing] that would have offended Rab,' while John Grigg in the *Spectator* was specially critical of 'shoddy editing'. This saddened me almost as much as the heartbreaking appearance of the book just eight days after Rab's death. John Grigg's article was headed 'Rab's Last Words.' He began:

Lord Butler of Saffron Walden was, as everyone agrees, a man of rare intelligence and fascination. He brought to politics, in a degree perhaps unmatched this century, those qualities which people like to describe, for praise or blame, as donnish. And in the last phase of his career he returned the compliment by bringing his great political experience into the academic world, as Master of Trinity College, Cambridge . . . Now, posthumously, we have a collection of his biographical essays, in which the autobiographical element remains strong . . . The essays are of uneven merit, but two or three are outstanding and all have Rab's distinctive flavour, which is both a delight and a poignant reminder of what we have lost.

This summer of 1981 the doctors felt the journey to Mull would be too strenuous and we went by car to Aldeburgh instead. I had omitted to look at the map before we started, being busy packing for our three weeks' stay, and neither had Rab. As I drove through the maze of Essex and Suffolk lanes, Rab said, 'It's quite easy, just drive towards the sea.' We had a delicious bedroom and bathroom on the ground floor of the hotel, with windows looking onto the sea, which sparkled at us from across the shingle beach only yards away. On this beach we spent peaceful hours reading to the sound of the waves or drove into the exquisite country around Aldeburgh.

One whole drowsy hot day (it was fine weather throughout our visit) we spent sitting by the river Alde behind the Maltings at Snape. The river widens as it runs towards the sea, so that we watched the sails of boats beyond the reeds, lazily floating by beneath a perfect summer sky, while through our binoculars we picked out tiny reed-buntings and a heron as immobile as ourselves. It was a magical time. Our old friends, Gladwyn and Cynthia Jebb drove over from their Suffolk home to dine with us, and Bishop Allison, now retired as Bishop of Winchester and living in Aldeburgh, came with his wife to dinner. Reading memoirs and biographies I have always been saddened by the inevitable running down towards the end of life, the letting go, the loosening of links and of things that make life dear. As a girl I was irritated by Browning's Rabbi ben Ezra into whose mouth he puts the words:

> Grow old along with me!
> The best is yet to be,
> The last of life, for which the first was made!

Foolish old man, I thought, how does he know what is yet to be?

And then one day, on 1 October to be exact, within two months and one week of his seventy-ninth birthday, Rab said the most marvellous thing to me, so marvellous that I immediately wrote it in my diary. He said: 'I am very interested in the *romance* of marriage. If you love someone, you don't notice or mind anything. It is the most wonderful institution if interpreted properly.' I set this down as a sort of testimony to old age . . .

Meanwhile summer was becoming autumn, but not before Rab said, 'There is much mystery in the beauty of Spencers – that dove cooing.' It was as though all his senses quickened as his physical powers failed. I remember mourning his lost health as, alone in the garden, I sadly picked the dahlias, flowers which I hate, and then pulling myself up with the thought, 'But you have him *here*.'

On 21 October we celebrated our twenty-second wedding anniversary with champagne and messages from our combined families of ten children. The autumn weather was fine and I find in my diary Rab saying, 'The trees are beautiful as a dream – I am quite happy with my trees and you,' and again an entry when we went up the park to discuss planting more trees, 'Now I am getting better. I hope I am getting better for your sake.'

On 4 November he went to Grilions for what proved to be the last time. I drove with him in the taxi to Grosvenor House, where the members then dined, and went up in the lift with him, to the amusement of Pat Dean and Harold Caccia, as I appeared to be invading their male stronghold. I dined below in a restaurant to enable me to escort him, in a happy mood, home to the flat. Next day was another 'last time', when he presided as President of the National Association for Mental Health at a luncheon in the Café Royal, attended by Princess

Alexandra, their Patron. He managed this with his old skill. Throughout his career he had given much time and care to societies connected
with mental health.

The last official function, which he performed this November, was to
present his portrait (painted by Robert Tollast in the 1960s) to St Mary's
Roman Catholic College of Higher Education. This is housed in Horace
Walpole's enchanting extravaganza, Strawberry Hill in Twickenham; I
was delighted at the chance to see it. We drove from the flat and Rab was
given a rest on arrival in Horace Walpole's bedroom, used by the
Principal as his study. This tiny room was panelled with Gothic arches,
picked out in blue and white. He was pushed in a wheelchair to the hall
of the College where, in spite of some difficulty with his breathing, he
unveiled his portrait and made his speech most gallantly. Afterwards
the students clustered round his chair and plied him with questions:
there was always great empathy between Rab and the young. Another
rest was followed by drinks in Walpole's own library, when he
commented, 'Gin and tonic – good. The Church of England would have
given us sherry.' The Principal entertained us, with many of his staff, to
dinner at the early hour of 6.30 to suit Rab, where, seated, he held the
table hanging on his words. He spoke about education in general, and
conducted a discussion which kept the company fascinated until we left
at 8.30 p.m.

The cruel winter of 1981–2 closed down on us at the beginning of
December, keeping us frozen in its grip of ice and snow for six weeks,
during which time it was impossible for Rab to leave the house. My
sorrow at its effect on his health was as bitter as the cold. However, we
decided to go by ship to South Africa in the New Year, and pored over
the brochures of life on board in the sun.

Alas, by January it became clear that the journey would be beyond his
strength. But still I continued to hope; while he was beside me, I could
do no other.

Then, at the beginning of March, came the end of hope, when the
doctor told me (but not Rab) that I must face the awful truth. During
this last week, Perina came again to run the house and see to the meals,
allowing me to be continuously with him in his room. She was an
enormous support.

I had never been able to discuss religion with Rab; he had no time for
my doubts and worries, brushing them aside as irrelevant. I am sure

that this attitude was the result of his own quiet faith. He was brought up to believe in the teachings of the Church and, as far as I am aware, never deviated from them. Why, therefore, bother to discuss something so certain and so simple? His own life was lived according to the highest Christian principles, and I am certain that these were deeply held by him from first to last, without the necessity of discussion or debate.

Harry Williams was to say of him (in his address at the service in Westminster Abbey in April), 'Behind that immense subtlety of mind and manoeuvre, so characteristic of Rab, there lay a conviction, simple yet profound, to which I believe he totally dedicated himself. It could be summed up in some well-known words from the Gospels: "A house divided against itself cannot stand." '

The nearest we ever got, he and I, to talking about 'Church' matters was during one of his last days, when I was sitting on his bed, since he had asked to look at my wedding-ring and he suddenly said, 'Read me all the hymns by Cowper in the *Ancient and Modern.*' William Cowper had written his favourite hymn, 'God moves in a mysterious way', which he had quoted during his first Budget Speech, exhorting the Commons with the line, 'Ye fearful saints, fresh courage take.'

On 8 March he became unconscious, although his eyes remained open. I sat beside him all that day, holding his hand and telling him how I loved him. Richard sat holding his other hand at intervals, and the rest of his children and mine gathered about us; I was unaware of all else but Rab. Christopher came from London. He prayed beside him and, if ever prayer meant something, it did so then. Afterwards Richard said to me, 'I don't think Papa heard what you were saying, but when Chris said "The Lord's Prayer" he seemed to register it.'

All that day his breathing sounded to me like waves on a rock-bound coast, until evening when, as I was preparing to lie down beside him for the night, it changed. The nurse summoned Richard. Christopher was also in the room, and my two daughters came to cling to me as, at 11.15, he died.

Grief is a house of many rooms. One which you enter brings a sense of total incomprehension. How is it possible that I am here and he is not, that I smell this flower, hear this bird singing, and he does not?

But I was lucky in my children, and his, who surrounded me with love and sympathy. I shall always remember the feeling of deep compassion which William conveyed with the two syllables 'Mama', spoken on the telephone across the world from Hong Kong. Of all the thousand and more letters which came at his death, the one that comforted me most was from a back-bench colleague in the House of Commons. He wrote: 'I hope you realize how happy you made him.' If this is true, it is something to live on for the rest of my life.

INDEX

INDEX